RETIREMENT BUCKET LIST PLAYBOOK

AN EASY, HOLISTIC AND BUDGET-FRIENDLY GUIDE TO JOYFUL ADVENTURES, DEEPER RELATIONSHIPS AND VIBRANT LIVING

ELIZA GOLDING

TABLE OF CONTENTS

INTRODUCTION

FINDERS KEEPERS

My friend Dawn and I were savoring our hot coffee at her kitchen table one sunny morning when she shared a deeply personal insight that captured my attention. "You know," she said, her eyes gazing into the horizon, "I used to think of retirement as endless days lounging on sun-drenched beaches, sipping piña coladas. But it's been way more exciting and meaningful than that!" She paused, relishing the aroma of the coffee. "In retirement, I found myself in ways I never expected."

With a sparkle in her eyes, Dawn continued, "Retirement has given me the chance to redefine my life and priorities, and in many ways, I've discovered more freedom and fulfillment than I ever imagined."

Dawn revealed how stepping away from her career liberated her from all the everyday pressures. She laughed about finally ditching her obsessive need for everything to be spotless and tidy. "It's OK for things to be a little messy," she said with relief. "I can actually enjoy my space instead of stressing about it!"

But that was just the beginning. Dawn explained how she filled her days with work that excited her and allowed her to set her own schedule. This reignited her passion and gave her a sense of purpose again. Taking her health more seriously, she took up running and developed a love for nutritious meals. She wanted to stay active and fit so she wouldn't be a burden to her kids down the line. And with travel now at the forefront of her plans, she was determined to explore the world before she turned 70.

Dawn's words echoed in my mind long after our conversation ended, and it hit me that retirement isn't just an extended break or a passive, declining phase of life. On the contrary, it can be an entirely new chapter brimming with adventure and opportunities, free from the constraints of traditional work life and allowing us to live boldly on our own terms.

Inspired by her journey and refreshing outlook, I felt a calling to share this insight with others. It led me to write this book to encourage you to explore your path to happiness, find yourself, and live life to the fullest.

Welcome to the Retirement Bucket List Playbook.

This book is for you, whether you're fully, partially, or getting ready for retirement. As a semi-retiree, I understand the unique challenges and opportunities that come with this stage of life and am here to help you navigate them.

This isn't your typical retirement guide. I'm not just handing you a list of travel destinations, hobbies or things to do. Instead, I'm presenting a holistic, budget-friendly approach that emphasizes personal growth, vibrant living, and yes, some unexpected adventures.

Whether you want to learn new skills, forge deeper connections or make unforgettable memories, this playbook is designed to help you enrich your retirement. Think of it as an adventure map that guides you toward your dreams and goals. The activities and ideas on our bucket list open doors to priceless memories and experiences. These might be once-in-a-lifetime opportunities, or ordinary moments that hold special meaning.

To simplify things, I've structured the book around a catchy acronym that embodies the core message of this book. Each component represents a vital element of your retirement journey, ensuring that you have a clear path forward. Expect to find practical tools, handy checklists and budget-friendly tips in these pages so you're well-equipped to pursue your retirement dreams. But it's not a one-way street. I've included interactive components like questions, challenges, and real-life scenarios to inspire you to take action.

Ready for your retirement adventure? Hop on in...

CHAPTER 1
REDISCOVERING PURPOSE AND PASSION

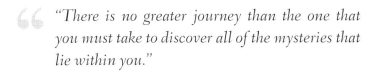

"There is no greater journey than the one that you must take to discover all of the mysteries that lie within you."

MICHELLE SANDLIN

Life has a funny way of throwing curveballs. Take my neighbor, Joshua, for instance. After four decades of proudly wearing his hard hat and dedicating himself to his craft, he retired. The routine that had structured his life vanished, leaving him in contemplation in his backyard. Gazing over the lawn he had meticulously maintained, he pondered, "What now?". During one of our conversations over our common fence, he shared with me, his voice tinged with uncertainty, that he felt adrift, like a ship without a sail.

Joshua's story isn't unique; it's as old as time. Many of us have spent years, even decades, defining ourselves through our careers. But what happens when the office door closes for the last time, and you hang up your work boots forever? Suddenly, that title on your business card doesn't fit anymore. It's like trying to wear a suit that's two sizes too small.

In this chapter, we'll peel back the layers of your career-defined identity to uncover the broader sense of self waiting to emerge. While our jobs have given us purpose and structure, retirement invites us to redefine what purpose means. Now, there are no more reports to file, meetings to attend, or deadlines to beat. It's time to transition from a structured, career-based identity to one that's expansive and full of promise.

FROM CAREER TO CALLING

Let's face it: You've spent much of your life in the working world, where job roles dictate much of your day-to-day existence. The job titles, the office cubicles, the daily grind—all these elements shaped who you were. But roles and titles are just parts of life, not the whole story. The core of who you are remains intact when you retire, and now you have the space to discover what makes you tick beyond the confines of a job description. You have the space to redefine your purpose and lead a purpose-driven retirement.

So, what exactly is a purpose-driven lifestyle in retirement? It's one where you live with intention and make choices that align with your values and passions. You wake up each day with zest and anticipation rather than dread. Purpose and passion may intersect, but they're not synonymous. Passion is your enthusiasm for certain activities, while purpose is the broader mission that drives you. Think of it like this: purpose is the map, and passion is the gas in your tank.

Having a clear purpose can help maintain life satisfaction. Research shows that retirees who embrace a sense of purpose often experience improved mental and physical health. They are less likely to feel bored, lonely or depressed. When you know what you're working towards, every day becomes an opportunity to contribute to something greater than yourself.

Reflecting on past roles can be a valuable exercise. What tasks brought you joy? What aspects of your career made you feel fulfilled? These reflections can act as a compass, guiding you toward your next chapter. Your career may have been a significant part of your life, but it doesn't have to define your future.

Exploring opportunities for meaningful engagement can help you redefine your sense of purpose. For instance, mentoring or coaching in areas of your expertise can offer a renewed sense of fulfillment. Sharing your lifetime of wisdom and knowledge benefits others and enhances your self-esteem. Engaging in community service or advocacy allows you to contribute to society meaningfully, bridging the gap between your past contributions and future endeavors.

Identifying your calling requires introspection and discovery. Life mapping exercises can be a helpful tool in this process. Life mapping is a technique where you create a visual representation of key events, milestones and experiences you've encountered throughout your life. By assembling a timeline, you can gain insight into your personal journey, identify patterns, and plan for the future. In essence, it's a graphic depiction of your life story.

Start by jotting down the activities that bring you joy, the skills you've honed over the years, and the passions you've nurtured. Then, look for patterns and connections. What stands out? What are the common threads that tie your experiences together? Identifying transferable skills and passions can guide you in crafting a retirement plan that aligns with your core values.

I'd like to share a few stories of individuals who have successfully transitioned from careers to fulfilling new roles. One of them is Chloe. After retiring as a pharmacist, she found herself baking pies in her kitchen, a hobby she had always loved but never had time for. What started as a way to pass the time turned into a thriving business at the local farmer's market, where she sold pies and connected with her community in ways she had never imagined.

Then there's Sunny, a high school teacher who devoted decades to educating young minds. Upon retirement, he discovered a new avenue to impart wisdom by becoming a mentor to young entrepreneurs. Leveraging his extensive experience in teaching, planning and guiding, Sunny now helps these budding business owners navigate the complexities of entrepreneurship. This transition into mentoring reignited Sunny's passion for educating and gave him a sense of fulfillment. Through sharing his knowledge and experience, he continues to impact the lives of others, proving that one's influence can extend far beyond traditional career paths.

These are just two of the many stories illustrating the diverse pathways to finding a calling and each individual's unique challenges. Some encountered self-doubt, while others struggled with the fear of the unknown. Yet, by staying open to new possibilities, they discovered new passions and redefined their purpose in life.

Now, it's your turn. What will your next chapter look like? Will you become a mentor, a community advocate, or an artist? The possibilities are endless. As you stand at the threshold of this new phase, remember that it's never too late to explore new identities and challenges. Embrace the freedom that comes with retirement, and let your passions guide you toward a fulfilling and purposeful life.

Life Mapping and Reflection

Grab a piece of paper and a pen. Draw a life timeline, marking significant events, roles and achievements. Next to each point, note what you enjoyed most about those experiences. What skills did you develop? What passions did you ignite? Look for patterns and themes. Reflect on how these experiences have shaped who you are today and how they can inform your future pursuits.

On this introspective journey, remember that retirement is a fresh start—a chance to change your story!

WHAT TRULY MATTERS

Let's explore what matters as you step into this new phase of life. You've spent years juggling responsibilities, meeting deadlines, and playing countless roles. Now, it's your chance to explore new roles and identities that resonate with your interests and bring fulfillment. What would these new roles be? The world is your oyster, and there are gems waiting for you to unearth.

Creativity is an area with limitless possibilities for finding joy and expression. Many of us have hidden artistic talents that never got their deserved attention. Retirement is the perfect time to dust off those paintbrushes, pick up a musical instrument, or try writing. Artistic endeavors allow us to create beautiful things and nurture our souls. They offer a chance to express emotions, tell stories, and leave a piece of yourself in everything you create. It's therapeutic, rewarding and most importantly, fun.

And if you find yourself inspired by new places, purposeful travel can broaden your horizons and enrich your life. Traveling isn't just about ticking off destinations; it's about seeking experiences that offer more profound meaning and learning opportunities. Whether it's a cultural exchange, a volunteer trip, or simply exploring a new city, travel can open your eyes to different ways of living and thinking. It's an invitation to step out of your comfort zone and embrace the world's diversity.

Speaking of embracing the world, let's not forget about our health and energy—two critical considerations in our retirement life. One of the best things you can do for yourself is to engage in low-impact exercises. They're gentle on the body yet effective in improving flexibility, strength and balance. Think of activities like yoga, taiqi, or even a brisk morning walk in the park. These exercises keep you fit and offer a moment of peace and reflection. They help you connect with your body, relieve stress and balance your mind and body.

Incorporating mindfulness and relaxation techniques into your daily routine can work wonders alongside physical exercise. Practices like meditation, deep breathing, or simply spending a few quiet moments in nature can reduce stress and enhance mental clarity. They provide a sanctuary for your mind, helping you navigate life's ups and downs gracefully and efficiently.

As we talk about nurturing ourselves, let's consider the incredible opportunity to share wisdom and knowledge with the next generation. You've accumulated a lifetime of invaluable experiences, lessons, and insights. Mentorship offers you the chance to guide and inspire younger generations. You can pass on the torch, share your journey and empower others to forge their paths.

The fulfillment derived from teaching and sharing knowledge is unparalleled. It's a two-way street where you learn as much as you teach, gaining new perspectives and insights. There's something profoundly rewarding about seeing someone flourish under your guidance, knowing that you've played a part in their success.

Equally rewarding is engaging with your local community through volunteering. When you give back to society, you connect with others and find purpose. Whether mentoring children, assisting at a local animal shelter, or helping organize community events, volunteering can fill your days with joy and meaning. Imagine the smiles you inspire, the stories you share, and the lives you touch. Non-profit organizations are fantastic avenues for finding roles that align with your values. They offer a chance to use your skills meaningfully while contributing to causes you care deeply about. It's a role reversal where you become the guide, the mentor, and the inspiration for others.

And while you're busy uplifting others, don't forget to invest in yourself through lifelong learning. Retirement is an ideal time for intellectual and personal growth. It's a chance to explore new interests, acquire new skills and expand your knowledge. Whether enrolling in a community college course, attending workshops, or simply picking up a book on a curious topic, learning keeps the mind sharp and agile. It's an opportunity to feed your curiosity, challenge your intellect and stay engaged with the world.

The cognitive benefits of continuous learning throughout retirement are profound and multifaceted. A wealth of research underscores that learning new skills bolsters cognitive function and significantly enhances mental agility. This continual intellectual engagement is a vigorous workout for your brain, mirroring the effects of physical exercise on the body. It fortifies neural pathways, fosters the growth of new brain cells, and enhances the brain's plasticity, its ability to reorganize and adapt. Engaging in educational activities, whether formal or informal, keeps your mind sharp and ready for the adventures that lie ahead.

As we wrap up this discussion on finding what truly matters, remember that retirement is not just a phase of life. It's a time when you can explore new roles and nurture your mind, body and soul. Let your new-found calling and purpose guide you as you dive into creative pursuits, share your wisdom and explore the world. Stay curious, passionate and most importantly, be true to what matters most.

CHAPTER 2
THE W.I.S.E. RETIREMENT BUCKET LIST

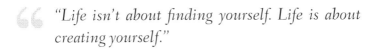 *"Life isn't about finding yourself. Life is about creating yourself."*

GEORGE BERNARD SHAW

Imagine standing in front of an old wooden chest, the kind you'd expect to find on a pirate ship, brimming with treasures waiting to be discovered. The W.I.S.E. bucket list is like this treasure chest, filled with curated ideas and recommendations for a memorable retirement. It's a fresh perspective on retirement, moving beyond the clichéd images of endless leisure and travel brochures.

Emphasizing personal growth, vibrant living and purpose-driven adventures, W.I.S.E. is organized under four simple, holistic and budget-conscious facets: Warm the Heart, Invigorate the Mind, Strengthen the Body, and Elevate the Soul.

Each facet contains thought-provoking pursuits and experiences that will infuse magic into your retirement years.

Make the W.I.S.E. bucket list your own by filling it with pursuits that align with your values, purpose and passions. Whether you're looking to learn a new skill, deepen your relationships or find joy in the everyday, this treasure chest would have something for you.

So, what makes an activity worthy of your bucket list? It's got to promise priceless memories and extraordinary experiences. It can be a once-in-a-lifetime opportunity or an ordinary moment infused with significant meaning.

Let's dive into Warm the Heart, the first facet of your treasure chest. Here, you'll find ideas that foster community—activities that will fill your days with laughter, love and shared experiences. Ever thought of joining a community theater as an actor or stagehand? Immerse yourself in the team spirit of bringing a story to life by doing so. Or you might consider hosting affordable dinner parties, where the joy of cooking is matched only by the delight of good company and conversation. These pastimes help you nurture relationships that support and uplift you.

Next, we move to Invigorate the Mind. This facet is like a mental gym, containing activities to keep your brain agile and curious. Embracing lifelong learning and finding joy in discoveries is key here. You could enroll in an accessible language class at your local library, where the thrill of learning a new vocabulary is enriched by the connections you make with fellow learners. Or you might prefer to dive into a book club, which amplifies the joy of reading through spirited debates and discussions.

Strengthen the Body is all about physical vitality and well-being. We'll explore hobbies that keep you fit and bring joy and relaxation. Think of gentle yoga classes at a community center, where your breath's rhythm matches your movements' calming flow. Or participate in pickleball, a social sport that offers a chance to make new friends while staying active. These pursuits nurture your body and help you find balance in strength and serenity.

Finally, we arrive at Elevate the Soul, the heart of the treasure chest. Here, the focus is on experiences that speak to your spirit, lift you and fill you with a sense of wonder and awe. Picture yourself exploring a local art museum, where each brushstroke tells a story, or volunteering at a wildlife sanctuary, where the beauty of nature becomes a part of your everyday life. These experiences help you connect with something greater than yourself and remind you of the beauty and magic around you.

We will explore the W.I.S.E. treasure chest in detail in the following pages, where you'll encounter engaging questions, challenges, and real-life stories to inspire you to take action and maximize your retirement years. For instance, I might ask you to plan a budget-friendly trip, or think about how you can incorporate a new skill into your daily routine. Whether you're reflecting on your goals, planning your next adventure, or simply savoring the small moments, these elements will support you in crafting a fulfilling retirement.

CHAPTER 3
W: WARM THE HEART

 "To love and be loved is to feel the sun from both sides."

DAVID VISCOTT

Let me take you to a small Pennsylvania town where Andrew and Catherine, both in their 60s, decided to reignite their social life by joining a local gardening club. They had been feeling like wilting flowers since their kids moved to different states, leaving them with a quiet house and too much time on their hands. One day, while sipping her morning coffee, Catherine stumbled upon a flyer for the gardening club and thought, "Why not?" The first meeting was a revelation; the couple found themselves amongst a group of fellow greenthumbs who shared horticultural tips, stories, laughter and companionship. Andrew and Catherine discovered that nurturing plants was only part of the joy; the friendships that bloomed were equally rewarding.

Social engagement is more than a casual pastime; it's a lifeline. Studies have shown that having strong social connections can do wonders for your health, both physically and mentally. Engaging with others can lead to longer life spans, reduced loneliness and even lower risks of cognitive decline and dementia. It's like watering your soul, keeping you vibrant and lively. As we grow older, maintaining these connections becomes even more critical. Yet, the hustle and bustle of life can sometimes make it challenging to stay connected. Enter the digital age, where technology becomes our trusty steed in the quest to remain socially active and engaged.

Warming the heart through social interaction, therefore, leads the way in the W.I.S.E. bucket list. This chapter will explore key activities that nurture relationships and foster community. In return, these activities support and uplift you, leading to a fulfilling and enriching retirement.

Finding
Your Community

Take a moment to jot down your interests and passions. Then, explore online platforms like Meetup or Facebook to find groups that align with your list. Attend a virtual event or join a group discussion, and note how these interactions make you feel.

Contact a local organization for volunteer opportunities, and reflect on the connections built. Find and nurture communities that resonate with your spirit.

INTERGENERATIONAL BONDING

Visualize the warmth of a bustling kitchen where you're showing your grandchild the secret to your famous apple pie. Or picture the wonder on their faces as you share tales from yesteryear that shaped your family history.

Intergenerational relationships offer a unique richness to our retirement life. Especially precious are relationships that involve teaching skills or trades to grandchildren, whether it's woodworking or knitting. Such pursuits allow us to 'pass the baton', bridging the past and the future and fostering a sense of pride and continuity. And why stop there? Reverse roles and have them teach you the wonders of modern technology, from navigating social media to using the latest gadgets. It's a delightful exchange that keeps you both engaged and connected.

Family-friendly activities are a treasure chest of opportunities to strengthen these bonds. Organize family game nights, where laughter flows as freely as the popcorn. Or host a movie marathon with classics that span generations, offering a shared cultural touchstone. Why not plan a picnic or a day at the beach when the sun is shining? The simple joys of nature can create lasting memories. And for those looking to make an epic adventure, consider a "grandcation" where you and the grandkids embark on a trip designed to explore, learn and grow together. Whether it's a camping trip in the great outdoors or a visit to a historical site, these experiences are the building blocks of cherished memories.

Regular family gatherings are paramount. Setting traditions like annual family reunions or holiday celebrations helps maintain those vital connections. But why wait for a special occasion? Monthly family dinners or potlucks bring everyone together, allowing all to share their stories and strengthen relationships. These gatherings reinforce familial bonds and ensure that no matter where life takes you, there's always a sense of belonging and unity waiting at home.

Friendships, too, deserve nurturing. Regular phone calls or coffee dates keep friendships vibrant, transforming acquaintances into lifelong companions. Small gestures can make a significant impact! Remembering a friend's birthday or celebrating their achievements brings joy and strengthens your bonds. These thoughtful acts show you care and create lasting connections that enrich our lives. Group vacations or weekend getaways provide a chance to escape routine and explore new horizons together. Whether it's a road trip to a nearby town or a weekend retreat in the mountains, these adventures offer a shared experience that strengthens ties.

Intergenerational relationships and friendships are the heartbeats of a fulfilling life. They remind us of where we've been, enrich where we are, and inspire where we're going. Sharing your wisdom, learning from the younger generations, and making time for those you cherish create a life full of warmth, laughter and love.

Grandcationing Practical Tips

Traveling smart (and stress-free) with the grandkids:

- Bring an authorization letter from the parents that permits you to travel with their children.

- Choose a child-friendly destination.

- Set ground rules regarding behavior and boundaries.

- Carry copies of crucial documents such as the kids' identification.

- Agree on a method of communication with the parents during the trip.

- Talk to the parents about any allergies or medical conditions the children may have.

- Review emergency procedures with the parents. Ensure you have their contact information, and local emergency contacts.

- Capture the moments: Take pictures! After the trip, consider creating a scrapbook together.

A VIBRANT COMMUNITY NETWORK

Imagine the joy of being part of a lively book club where laughter echoes off the walls or perhaps a gardening society where you swap seedlings and stories in equal measure. Joining clubs and groups can lift your spirits, especially when an empty nest and quiet surroundings make you crave connection. The rise of solo agers due to fewer marriages and smaller family sizes means many of us seek new tribes later in life. These groups become communities of shared interests and experiences, where friendships and a sense of belonging can blossom. Whether it's a chess circle where strategic minds meet over a game board or a knitting club that spins yarns and tales in tandem, the connections formed are invaluable. They combat loneliness and build a vibrant social network that enriches your days.

Finding the right group, however, can feel like searching for a needle in a haystack. Start by exploring local community centers and libraries, which often host clubs and meetings on various topics. Platforms like Meetup and Facebook can be excellent resources, connecting you to gatherings that align with your interests and values. Finding a group that resonates with your passions and where you feel comfortable and appreciated is critical. Once you find your niche, dive in. Participate actively, and let your voice be heard. Volunteering for group events or stepping into a leadership role can deepen your involvement and enrich your experience. Regular attendance and engagement are vital for maximizing the benefits of these connections. The more you put into a group, the more you'll get out of it.

But what if you can't find the right group? Consider starting your own. If the local scene lacks a neighborhood walking group, why not be the one to organize it? A monthly board game night can be a great way to bring people together for fun and fellowship. Starting a group might seem daunting, but it's an opportunity to create a space that reflects your interests and fosters new friendships. Take the initiative to fill the gaps and meet the needs of your community.

The beauty of building a vibrant community network lies in its ability to transform strangers into friends and acquaintances into companions. Find a tribe that shares your joys, supports you through life's challenges and celebrates your victories. Whether you're rekindling old passions or exploring new ones, these connections are crucial for leading a fulfilling and meaningful life. They remind us that we're never truly alone; there's always a community waiting to welcome us with open arms.

MEANINGFUL CONNECTIONS THROUGH VOLUNTEERING

Volunteering is like giving a hug to your community—it's warm, fulfilling, and leaves everyone feeling a bit better. When you step into the world of volunteering, you are not only offering your time but also building bridges with fellow volunteers and creating a network of friends who share your passion for making a difference. Each project you engage in contributes to a larger picture, offering a sense of accomplishment and purpose. It's like baking a cake, where every ingredient, every minute spent, adds up to something rewarding.

There are diverse volunteering opportunities out there. Examples include organizing supplies at food banks, serving meals at local soup kitchens, assisting in wildlife conservation efforts, caring for the sick at hospitals, and nurturing our furry friends at animal shelters. The key is finding an opportunity that aligns with your skills and passions and makes your heart sing. The impact of your actions will ripple through the community, bringing people closer and strengthening bonds.

Choosing the right volunteer role involves introspection. Start by identifying organizations that match your values and places where your contributions will feel meaningful.

Consider the time commitment required, ensuring it fits comfortably within your schedule. It would help if you initially dipped your toes into short-term projects, gradually transitioning into long-term commitments as you find rhythm. Ongoing projects provide the opportunity to build lasting relationships and witness the growth and flourishing of your efforts over time. Examples include community gardening or mentoring youth through educational programs.

Long-term volunteer efforts can be gratifying. They allow you to witness the evolution of a project and the positive changes you're helping to foster. Mentoring youth, for instance, offers a unique opportunity to shape and guide the next generation, imparting wisdom and knowledge that can ignite a spark in young minds. Community garden initiatives beautify neighborhoods, provide fresh produce, and foster a sense of camaraderie among participants. These projects, with their moments of growth, learning and shared victories, will warm your heart long after completion.

Volunteering is a two-way street where you give and receive, finding joy in the smiles and gratitude of those you help. So, take a moment to explore the possibilities.

BRINGING PEOPLE TOGETHER THROUGH EVENT HOSTING

Hosting events is another delightful way to bring people together. Whether it's a dinner party, a seasonal barbecue or a simple potluck, gatherings create opportunities for connection and community building. Great hosts don't just set a table or prepare a meal; they craft a space where people feel welcomed and valued. A warm greeting at the door, a cozy atmosphere and a playlist that sets the mood are just the beginning. When guests feel at ease, meaningful conversations flow naturally, deepening connections and creating memories long after the party.

You could host a themed dinner party, where guests dress in their favorite decade and share stories from that era. Or organize a potluck, where each dish brings a taste of someone's heritage to the table, sparking conversations about family traditions and culinary secrets. Seasonal celebrations, like a summer barbecue with grilled delights wafting through the air or a holiday party adorned with twinkling lights, offer a delightful way to mark the changing seasons with friends and family.

Planning a successful event requires organization and a dash of creativity. Start by sending out invitations that reflect the theme and excitement of the occasion. Whether it's a handwritten note or a digital invite, make sure it communicates the date, time and any special instructions. Collecting RSVPs helps with planning and ensures you're prepared for the number of guests. Preparing food and entertainment in advance allows you to relax and enjoy the event alongside your guests. A well-curated playlist or a simple game can keep the energy lively and engaging.

Inclusivity is the heart of any gathering. Consider the dietary restrictions and accessibility needs of your guests, ensuring that everyone feels comfortable and catered to. If Uncle Joe is lactose intolerant, that cheese platter could include dairy-free options. Encourage diverse participation by inviting guests from different circles of your life. It's a chance to introduce your book club friends to your pickleball pals, creating an eclectic blend of perspectives and stories—the beauty of hosting lies in creating a space where everyone feels seen and heard.

Hosting events offers a unique opportunity to unite people and create moments that linger long after the last guest has left, memories that are cherished and revisited with a smile. Whether it's the clinking of glasses at a dinner party or the shared laughter around a bonfire, these gatherings celebrate life's simple joys, a reminder of the connections that enrich our lives. Creating opportunities for connection and community building through hosting is a gift that brings warmth, happiness and a sense of belonging to everyone involved.

GROUP TRAVEL, SHARED ADVENTURES

Ever wonder what it's like to travel with others? Well, now's the time to give it a go. Experience the thrill of discovering new places alongside companions who share your wonder. You might even form life-changing bonds that you never expected.

There's something magical about sharing the experience of a sunset over a distant mountain or the laughter that echoes through a bustling market. Traveling with others can amplify these moments, transforming a simple trip into an adventure filled with camaraderie. When you travel in a group, costs and responsibilities become shared, making the journey more affordable and less stressful. You can split the cost of accommodations, transportation and even meals while sharing the load of planning and logistics. It's like having a team where each member brings their strengths, turning the trip into a communal effort where everyone contributes to the fun and success.

Planning a group trip requires a bit of coordination, but the rewards are well worth the effort. Start by choosing destinations that appeal to all group members, ensuring everyone has a say in the itinerary. This collaborative approach builds excitement and ensures that the trip caters to diverse interests. Once you've settled on a destination, set a collective budget for transportation, accommodation and activities. Creating an itinerary together allows for flexibility and ensures everyone gets to experience something they love. It involves negotiation and compromise, where every voice is heard and valued, resulting in a trip that reflects the group's collective desires and dreams.

Communication is the cornerstone of successful group travel. Establishing clear roles and responsibilities is essential to avoid any last-minute surprises or misunderstandings. Decide who will handle bookings, who will research activities, and who will be the designated navigator. Setting expectations and preferences in advance can prevent conflicts and ensure everyone is on the same page. Discuss preferences for pace, dining options and activities to create a harmonious experience where everyone feels comfortable and included. A little planning goes a long way in ensuring the trip runs smoothly, and everyone returns with a smile and cherished memories.

Finding travel companions might seem daunting, but many avenues exist to explore. You can start by reaching out to friends or family who share your wanderlust, proposing the idea of a group getaway. If your circle is more of the couch potato variety, consider joining travel clubs or tours designed for seniors and retirees. These organizations often organize group trips, providing a ready-made community of fellow travelers eager to explore the world with you. These groups offer many opportunities to connect with like-minded adventurers, from local travel meetups to organized tours.

Group travel is more than just seeing new places; it offers shared experiences and the prospect of creating bonds and friendships. Think of the laughter over a shared meal, the stories told on a long bus ride, and the collective wonder at a breathtaking view. These experiences, shared with those who traveled alongside you, create a rich album of memories.

DIGITAL COMMUNITIES, GLOBAL PERSPECTIVES

Picture this: you're sitting in the comfort of your living room, participating in a virtual cooking class, or discussing the latest bestseller with people across the globe through an online book club. In today's interconnected world, this can be your reality.

Embracing technology can be a powerful way to maintain connections and combat feelings of isolation. The Internet has made the world smaller, allowing us to be part of communities that transcend geographical boundaries. In fact, digital communities have become integral to staying connected, especially for retirees who are more tech-savvy than ever.

Social media and online forums offer many opportunities to engage with others who share your interests and passions. Whether it's a forum dedicated to vintage car enthusiasts or a virtual support group for retirees navigating similar challenges, the digital landscape has something for everyone. It's like having a world of possibilities at your fingertips, ready to explore at your own pace and convenience.

The benefits of engaging online are numerous. One of the most appealing aspects is the flexibility it offers. You can participate from anywhere, whether lounging in your favorite chair or sipping coffee at a local café with Wi-Fi. This level of accessibility means you're never more than a few clicks away from connecting with a global community. Engaging with people from different backgrounds and cultures broadens your horizons and fosters a sense of belonging. It's a chance to share experiences, learn from others, and build connections that enrich your life. The digital realm provides a platform where geographical boundaries fade away, allowing friendships to flourish without distance constraints.

Finding and joining digital communities might seem daunting, but it's easier than you think. Start by exploring social media platforms like Facebook, Reddit or Meetup, where you can find groups tailored to almost any interest imaginable. From knitting circles to movie fanatics, there's a community waiting to welcome you.

Specialized forums and websites can also be treasure troves of information and interaction. Whether you want to learn more about gardening or connect with fellow travelers, a quick search can lead you to vibrant online spaces filled with like-minded individuals. Be sure also to check out dedicated senior-focused platforms like AARP, Senior Planet, Silversurfers and Buzz50. The key is to dive in and explore, allowing your curiosity to guide you to communities that resonate with you.

Once you've found your digital tribe, maintaining those online relationships is essential. Regular participation in discussions or activities keeps you engaged and helps you build meaningful connections. Instead of just logging in and lurking, consider contributing your voice and sharing your experiences. Building friendships through shared interests creates a sense of solidarity and support.

Digital communities can offer encouragement, advice and companionship, providing a virtual network that enriches your daily life. The friendships you cultivate online can become as valuable and fulfilling as those formed in person, offering a space where you're valued and understood.

WISDOM AND LEGACY FOR THE NEXT GENERATION

Imparting your wisdom and leaving a legacy is a noble pathway to warm your heart during retirement. By guiding and inspiring the next generation, you find a renewed sense of purpose and a chance to impart knowledge that might change a life.

Joining mentorship programs in local schools allows you to step into this role and make a tangible difference. Professional organizations often seek mentors with rich experiences, and you have a lifetime of wisdom to share. Imagine the impact of your guidance on someone just starting their career. The ripple effect of your insights can shape the leaders of tomorrow.

Another beautiful way to share your journey with future generations is by writing a memoir or personal blog that captures the essence of your experiences and the wisdom you've gathered, leaving a legacy that reflects your values and life's work. It's like leaving a map for others, guiding them through the paths you've traveled, the challenges you've faced and the triumphs you've celebrated. Establishing scholarships or community awards in your name can also be a lasting testament to your commitment to education and community service. These initiatives can continue to impact lives long after you've moved on to new adventures, creating a legacy that resonates with your values and passions.

Intergenerational activities foster connections that transcend age, meaningfully uniting family members and the community. Organizing family storytelling sessions can create a sense of shared history, where tales from the past meet the curiosity of the present. Experience the joy of watching your grandchildren's faces light up as they hear about the world you grew up in, the places you've been, and the people you've met. Participating in community gardening projects can also bridge generations, offering a chance to work together towards a common goal and re-establishing bonds.

Teaching and sharing knowledge is a path to personal growth and fulfillment. Offering workshops or classes based on your professional expertise allows you to continue contributing to your field, nurturing the next generation of professionals. Whether it's a cooking class, a finance seminar or a creative writing workshop, your insights can inspire and empower others. Volunteering as a guest speaker at local events or organizations can also be incredibly rewarding. Sharing your experiences, challenges and successes can inspire others to chase their dreams with courage and determination. Knowledge, inspiration and hope will be the legacy you leave behind.

As you reflect on how to share your wisdom and leave a legacy, consider the impact of your actions on those who follow in your footsteps. Your stories and insights are treasures waiting to be shared.

CHAPTER 4
I: INVIGORATE THE MIND

 "Live as if you were to die tomorrow. Learn as if you were to live forever."

MAHATMA GANDHI

Su Zhen, a retired accountant from Shanghai, decided at age 70 to learn the art of calligraphy. Now, I know what you're thinking: calligraphy? Isn't that just fancy handwriting? Well, for Su Zhen, it became a gateway to a whole new world. She discovered not only the beauty in the brush strokes but also a meditative practice that sharpened her focus and renewed her zest for life. It was as if she had unlocked a secret garden within her mind, where creativity bloomed and worries faded.

Su Zhen's experience reminds us that it's never too late to invigorate our minds and enjoy learning something new. If, like her, your retirement goal is to keep your brain in tip-top shape, this chapter is for you. Let's delve into 'Invigorate the Mind', the second facet in the W.I.S.E. bucket list.

Keeping your mind sharp doesn't mean you have to solve quantum physics problems—unless that's your thing. All you need is to find activities that stimulate your brain, creating new neural pathways that help keep your mind agile and alert. Just like Su Zhen discovered her calling in calligraphy, you can find your path to mental wellness. You could engage in a heated chess game with a friend, where each move requires strategy and foresight. Or perhaps you're drawn to the world of puzzles, where each piece you fit is a tiny victory.

But let's not limit ourselves to traditional games and challenges. There's a universe of ways to keep your mental gears turning. Have you ever considered taking up a musical instrument, for instance? Even if the last time you played was a recorder in fourth grade, music is a remarkable tool for enhancing brain function. Playing a new instrument can improve memory and coordination, offering many benefits for your mind. Perhaps you'd like to dabble in painting or sculpture, where creativity knows no bounds? Art provides an outlet for self-expression and engages different parts of the brain, making it both therapeutic and stimulating.

Connecting with your community can also offer mental stimulation. Attend local lectures or join discussion groups where you can exchange ideas and explore new perspectives. This keeps your mind sharp plus allows you to bond with others who share your interests. What about joining a storytelling group where you can share your life's adventures and hear stories from others? Storytelling is a beautiful and creative way to enhance mental agility and social ties.

Invigorate your mind by finding what intrigues you and makes you feel alive. The important thing is to keep exploring, questioning, and discovering the possibilities within your reach.

Journaling Exercise

Putting ideas and thoughts onto paper:

Take a moment to reflect on activities that have intrigued you but perhaps felt out of reach. Consider what steps you might take to explore these interests further. Are there local classes you could join? Books you could read? People you could reach out to for guidance or mentorship?

Write all these down in a journal. There's no need to commit to a new hobby overnight. Let this exercise plant seeds of curiosity in you, and watch your exploratory ideas evolve.

ONLINE LEARNING: MASTERING NEW SKILLS

Sip your morning coffee while studying—right from your kitchen table! Thanks to technological advances, this is now possible through online learning.

Online learning has revolutionized how we acquire knowledge, offering opportunities at our fingertips. It's like having a personal university that runs on your schedule without the hassle of a commute or rigid timetable. Best part is, the online realm offers a wide array of subjects to explore—from coding, artificial intelligence and data science to design, art history and digital photography. You can study at your own pace, pausing when life gets busy and diving deep when curiosity strikes. This flexibility makes online classes perfect for retirees, allowing you to balance learning with other activities.

Platforms like Coursera and edX have opened their virtual doors to learners worldwide, offering courses from prestigious universities. You can explore ancient civilizations with a professor from Yale or delve into modern physics with an expert from MIT—all without leaving your living room. If you're more inclined towards creative or practical skills, Skillshare might be your platform of choice. You can find courses that cater to your artistic side, from watercolor painting to graphic design. The best part? Many of these courses are free or offer affordable options, ensuring lifelong learning doesn't have to break the bank.

Choosing the right course can feel like picking a book in a vast library. Start by considering your interests and goals, then explore course offerings that align with them. Reading course reviews and testimonials can provide valuable insights from fellow learners, helping you gauge the quality and relevance of the content. Evaluating the course content and instructor expertise is also crucial. A glance at the instructor's bio and course outline can tell if the course fits your learning style and objectives well. Here are some key features to look out for:

- **Varied course topics**: A diverse range of subjects, from hobbies such as gardening, painting and photography to practical skills like cooking, finance management, health and wellness, history and current events.
- **Personalized learning paths**: Options to customize learning experiences based on individual interests, prior knowledge and skill levels.
- **Bite-sized lessons**: Course content that is broken down into smaller, manageable lessons, allowing retirees to learn at their own pace.
- **User-friendly interface**: Simple navigation, large fonts and an intuitive design, ensuring ease of use for those who may not be tech-savvy.
- **Community features**: Discussion forums, group projects, and interactive elements to foster connections and collaboration with fellow learners, which can enhance motivation and engagement.
- **Video lectures**: Video-based courses with closed captioning, supporting visual learners and providing accessibility for those with hearing difficulties.

As lifelong learning is an ongoing discovery process, take the time to find classes that resonate with you. Consider setting learning goals to keep yourself motivated and on track. You might aim to learn a new skill every month or complete a series of courses on a specific topic. With clear goals, you will have a better sense of direction and accomplishment. Join online study groups or forums to enhance your learning experience, as these communities of like-minded individuals can share insights and encouragement, making learning more enjoyable.

Hot Tips: Top Learning Platforms

Explore these platforms for your learning adventure:

Coursera
www.coursera.org
Partners with universities to offer diverse courses with flexible learning paths, and degree and non-degree options.

AARP
www.aarp.org
Offers educational resources and online courses for older adults. Many resources are offered free to members.

Khan Academy
www.khanacademy.org
Offers free courses with interactive exercises and instructional videos.

Udemy
www.udemy.com
Hosts a vast library of over 155,000 courses on diverse topics and lifetime access.

Skillshare
www.skillshare.com
Focuses on creative skills, with a project-based and collaborative learning approach.

edX
www.edx.org
Offers courses from institutions like Harvard and MIT, with an option to earn certificates.

NB: Check out your local community colleges too. Many of them offer discounted or free courses for seniors.

LANGUAGE LEARNING: DOORWAY TO NEW CULTURES

Have you ever found yourself captivated by the lilting tones of Italian, the precise clicks of Xhosa, or the melodic flow of Hindi? Language is more than just words. It's a gateway to new worlds. Acquiring a new language opens the door to different cultures and traditions.

Learning a new language can be an exciting experience. It enhances your brain health by sharpening your memory and multitasking skills, providing a mental workout that keeps your mind sharp. But the benefits don't stop there. As you unravel the complexities of a foreign tongue, you gain insights into cultural nuances and traditions that enrich your understanding and appreciation of the world and its people.

How do you start this linguistic journey? The good news is there are many paths to choose from, each catering to different learning styles and preferences. If you enjoy a structured approach, consider enrolling in community college courses. These courses often offer the bonus of inter-acting with fellow students, making it a social experience. On the other hand, if you prefer a more flexible schedule, digital apps like Duolingo and Babbel are excellent compan-ions. They transform learning into a game-like experience, where each level conquered feels like a small victory. These apps allow you to practice on the go, turning mundane moments like waiting in line or sipping your morning coffee into opportunities for language practice.

But let's be honest: learning a language goes beyond textbooks and apps. To truly grasp a language, you need to immerse yourself in it. Consider joining language exchange meetups or clubs where you can practice with native speakers in a supportive environment. These gatherings provide real-world experience, allowing you to hone your conversational skills while making new friends.

Participating in cultural immersion programs can take your learning to the next level. These could be a language retreat in the countryside of France or a homestay with a family in Peru. Such experiences offer a chance to live and use a language in everyday contexts.

Once you've dipped your toes into the world of language learning, maintaining your skills becomes the next challenge. Regular conversations with native speakers are invaluable. They help you refine your pronunciation and gain confidence in your speech. Consider joining online language communities or finding a language buddy with whom you can chat regularly.

Watching films or reading books in your target language is another effective way to keep your skills sharp. Subtitles can be your training wheels, gradually weaning off as your comprehension improves. Integrate the language into your daily life and make it a natural part of your routine. Learning a language is a journey of discovery, where each word learned is a step closer to understanding the world.

TIME TRAVEL WITH BOOKS

Visualize a world where every book is a door to a different universe. You're not just turning pages but stepping into new realms. It's almost like time travel... one moment you're in the present, and the next, you're in ancient Rome, unraveling political intrigues; or perhaps you're in a dystopian future where robots rule the land. It's this diversity of genres that makes reading such an enriching experience.

Romance, fantasy, science fiction, mystery, horror, dystopian... there's a gamut of genres that can open your mind to new perspectives and ideas. If you've always stuck to mysteries, why not try a fantasy novel where magic is real, or a historical fiction that brings the past to life? Joining a book club can also add a new dimension to your reading. Experience the conversations, debates and fellowship that come with sharing stories and insights with fellow book lovers.

Set personal reading goals to transform your reading into an enjoyable challenge. You may aim to read a certain number of books each month or explore different themes and authors. Keeping a reading journal can be an excellent companion. It's a space to jot down your thoughts, reflect on book themes, and record the insights you gain from each book. Think of it as a scrapbook where you can revisit your literary adventures later and see how they've shaped your thinking and understanding.

Audiobooks and e-readers are two fantastic tools that have revolutionized how we read. Audiobooks, in particular, turn mundane tasks into opportunities for literary exploration.

You can be walking in the park while listening to a gripping thriller, or cooking dinner as an enchanting tale unfolds in your ears. It's multitasking at its finest, allowing you to enjoy stories while going about your day. E-readers are also a great tool, as they offer a personalized reading experience with adjustable text sizes, a blessing for those of us who struggle with fine print. They're lightweight and portable, perfect for taking your library on the go, whether you're traveling or simply lounging in your backyard.

Libraries and online resources are treasure chests waiting to be explored! Many libraries today offer free access to digital audiobooks and e-books through platforms like OverDrive and Libby. You can now have a library card that works 24/7, ready to lend you a book at the click of a button. If you love the classics, websites like Project Gutenberg provide free access to thousands of timeless literary works, from the romantic prose of Jane Austen to the philosophies of Fyodor Dostoevsky. These resources make reading accessible and convenient, ensuring you're never far from your next great read.

BRAIN GAMES FOR SHARP MINDS

As we age, it's natural for our cognitive functions to slow down, but that doesn't mean we have to let it happen without a fight. We can help delay age-related decline and maintain mental agility by keeping those brain neurons firing.

Brain games are an excellent challenge that stimulates your brain and keeps it agile. They are akin to giving your mind a good workout. An excellent example is solving puzzles and brain teasers. These are not just idle pastimes; they provide a satisfying mix of problem-solving and creativity. Strategy board games like chess or checkers can be the perfect companions. Each move demands foresight, strategy and a bit of cunning—all elements that keep your brain engaged. Plus, they're a great way to spend an afternoon with friends or family.

When choosing brain games, find activities that challenge your mind while being enjoyable. If you love history, perhaps historical trivia nights would be a hit. If numbers are your thing, indulge in a good sudoku or math puzzle. Also, rotating between different types of puzzles and games keeps things fresh and prevents boredom. One day, you might tackle a jigsaw puzzle, and the next, a logic riddle. The variety keeps your brain guessing, always on its toes.

Use brain games to nurture your mind and keep it vibrant. Remember, it's not just about winning—though that's always a nice bonus.

Beyond brain games, there are endless activities to stimulate your mind. Learning a new skill or hobby, for example, can be incredibly rewarding. Whether it's taking up knitting, painting or even learning to juggle, these activities engage different parts of your brain, challenging you to think in new ways. Another fantastic option is participating in trivia nights or quizzes. The thrill of recalling a random fact just in the nick of time almost always brings on the laughs and the bonding.

Now, let's talk about the social side of things. Cognitive health doesn't exist in a vacuum. Often, it's social interactions that enrich these activities. Joining a book club or discussion group offers a double benefit: mental stimulation and social engagement. The lively debates and exchanges of ideas can invigorate, sparking new thoughts and perspectives. Attending lectures or educational events provides similar benefits, opening doors to new knowledge while fostering connections with others who share your interests. Social cognitive activities remind us that learning and growing are best enjoyed together.

CREATIVE SIDE HUSTLES AND ENCORE CAREERS

The prospect of rediscovering passions and exploring new opportunities becomes an enticing possibility as retirement looms or once we retire. Have you considered turning a beloved hobby into a side hustle? Could your years of professional experience transition seamlessly into freelance work after you retire?

Picture yourself crafting and selling handmade goods, each piece a testament to your skill and creativity. Whether knitting scarves or crafting jewelry, your creations could find a home on platforms like Etsy, where artisans worldwide showcase their talents. If you, like me, have a knack for writing and editing, platforms like Upwork offer a space to connect with clients seeking your expertise, allowing you to earn an income while doing what you love.

The concept of encore careers is gaining traction among retirees who seek more than just leisure in their golden years. An encore career allows you to align work with your values and passions, offering fulfillment beyond a paycheck. You might choose to work part-time in a field you've always been curious about, or take on a role that allows you to give back to the community. The beauty of an encore career lies in its flexibility and the chance to explore interests that may have been sidelined during your primary career.

Transitioning into an encore career requires planning and introspection. Start by updating your resume to reflect your accomplishments and aspirations. Highlight transferable skills relevant to the new roles you're interested in. Invest in skill development through workshops or online courses, ensuring you're well-equipped for the new challenges ahead. Gain valuable insights and support by seeking mentorship or guidance from those in your desired field, or those who have successfully made similar transitions.

Balancing work and leisure is crucial to maintaining a fulfilling retirement. Flexible work arrangements can offer the best of both worlds, allowing you to enjoy the perks of employment without sacrificing personal time. Consider part-time roles or freelance projects that enable you to set your own hours and work from home. Prioritizing work-life harmony means being mindful of how you spend your time, ensuring that work doesn't overshadow leisure and relaxation. Retirement is about savoring the moments—like a quiet afternoon in the garden or a spirited game night with friends. Find the right balance to enjoy the fruits of your life's labor.

EMBRACING TECH FOR BUCKET LIST MANAGEMENT

Organizing your bucket list has never been easier in today's digital age. Remember the old days of scribbling notes on paper and losing them in the abyss of a drawer? Those days are behind us. Digital tools are your best friends when organizing and achieving your retirement dreams. Take Evernote, for instance. It's like having a virtual notebook at your fingertips, perfect for jotting down ideas, brainstorming your next adventure, or even keeping a diary of your experiences. With its seamless syncing across devices, your notes are never more than a click away, ensuring your plans stay organized no matter where you are.

If you crave more structure, Trello offers a visual feast for project management. Here, your bucket list can be organized as a series of cards, each representing a dream waiting to be fulfilled. Trello allows you to move these cards around, set deadlines, and even add checklists, turning your aspirations into actionable steps.

The beauty of digital planning tools lies in their ability to streamline the process of achieving your goals. Gone are the days of sticky notes and cluttered bulletin boards. With digital calendars, you can set reminders and deadlines, ensuring that your plans don't get lost in the shuffle of daily life. Plan that long-awaited trip to Italy with reminders to book flights, reserve accommodations and even start that packing list. You can easily share your plans with friends and family from these apps, allowing collaboration and input from them. This keeps your loved ones posted about your projects and ensures everyone is on the same page, whether the occasion is a family reunion or a solo adventure.

But which tools should you choose? The options might seem overwhelming, but fear not. Start with highly recommended ones like Monday.com for its customizable workflows and visual appeal; Asana for its simple interface and team collaboration features; Google Tasks for seamless integration with other Google products; and Basecamp for its user-friendly design. Then there's Google Keep, if you prefer a simple, straightforward approach to note-taking. It's like having a digital sticky note on your phone, perfect for jotting down quick ideas or reminders.

Experiment with different digital tools to find what works for you. Each offers unique features tailored to various needs and preferences. Customize these digital tools to fit your style, whether you're a visual thinker or someone who thrives on lists. Find what resonates with you and what makes planning a joy rather than a chore. The goal is to make your bucket list not just a dream but a reality.

Remember that keeping your brain engaged is not just about mental gymnastics but staying curious and open to new experiences, ideas and technologies. Next, we'll explore how to strengthen the body, ensuring you're ready for all the adventures your bucket list holds.

CHAPTER 5
S: STRENGTHEN THE BODY

 "Strength does not come from physical capacity. It comes from an indomitable will."

MAHATMA GANDHI

Rosniati, a remarkable woman from Jordan, decided at 68 to transform her health. Rosniati had spent years focused on her family, often neglecting her own well-being. One day, after struggling to climb stairs, she realized it was time for a change. With determination in her heart, she set out to improve her health one step at a time.

Rosniati began with simple morning walks around her neighborhood. As the days turned into weeks, those walks grew longer and faster. Soon, she added gentle stretching exercises to her routine, feeling her body become more limber and resilient. Her newfound energy was infectious, and it wasn't long before her friends joined her. This eventually became a small exercise group that met regularly to walk, stretch and chat.

Rosniati's story is a testament to the power of determination and the profound impact that even modest physical activity can have on our lives. This leads us to the third facet of W.I.S.E., 'Strengthen the Body'. If physical health and wellness are your top retirement priorities, read on.

As we enter our golden years, prioritizing our physical health becomes more critical. Regular physical activity is like an elixir that offers many benefits. According to the Centers for Disease Control and Prevention (CDC), regular physical activity can improve sleep quality, reduce feelings of anxiety, and even lower blood pressure. In the long term, it helps reduce the risk of chronic diseases such as heart disease, stroke and Type 2 diabetes while promoting bone health and enhancing balance and coordination.

The secret to regular physical activity is finding something you enjoy that fits seamlessly into your life. The options are endless, whether it's a morning walk, a swim at the local pool or even a dance class. The most important thing is to get moving and savor the strength and vitality it brings.

Diet plays a crucial role in maintaining health and wellness as well. A balanced diet supports physical health and longevity, ensuring you have the energy and nutrients to enjoy your retirement fully. Incorporating a variety of fruits and vegetables, whole grains and lean proteins into your meals can make all the difference. For instance, a breakfast of oatmeal with fresh berries, a lunch of grilled chicken salad, and a dinner of roasted vegetables with quinoa are all nutritious and delicious.

Staying hydrated is equally important, and something as simple as carrying a water bottle with you can help maintain hydration levels throughout the day. Meal planning can also be a valuable tool, helping you make smart food choices and ensuring a steady supply of nutritious meals. Cooking in batches can save time and effort while providing delicious, healthy options. Remember, eating well doesn't mean deprivation; you're nourishing your body and enjoying creating and savoring meals.

Reflections

Take a moment to reflect on your current lifestyle. What small changes might you make to incorporate more physical activity and healthy eating? What activities bring you joy and make you feel alive?

Jot down a few ideas in a journal, and set a simple goal for the week. Maybe it's trying a new recipe or walking in a park. Start small and build from there, creating habits that support your health and well-being.

As you embark on this journey to strengthen your body, remember that it's about progress, not perfection. This means you don't have to achieve all your health and fitness goals simultaneously. Taking small steps toward your desired outcome is okay. Find what works for you and celebrate each step forward, no matter how small. Whether you're inspired by Rosniati's story or want to carve out your own path, know that you have the power to create a life filled with vitality.

GENTLE EXERCISES TO STAY FIT AND ACTIVE

You're strolling through a local park, the morning sun casting a warm glow and a gentle breeze rustling through the trees. This isn't just a leisurely walk; it's a simple yet effective way to boost your flexibility, strength and balance without straining your body. Walking is a marvelous, low-impact exercise that can be tailored to suit your pace and preference. You might start with a few laps around the park, gradually increasing your distance as your confidence and stamina grow. Each step strengthens your muscles and lifts your spirits, offering a moment of peace in a busy world. And if you're feeling social, a walking buddy or a group can add a delightful fellowship to your routine.

If you seek a bit more structure, gentle yoga or taiqi classes offer a sanctuary of calm and focus. These practices encourage mindfulness and body awareness, guiding you through movements that enhance balance and flexibility. You'll find that the slow, deliberate poses and stretches can ease tension and promote relaxation. Picture yourself in a sunlit studio or even your living room, moving gracefully from one pose to another, your breath steady and your mind at ease. If you're new to these practices, many classes are tailored to beginners, ensuring you feel comfortable and supported.

But let's not stop there! Water aerobics is another fantastic option for those seeking joint-friendly workouts. This exercise not only provides a cardiovascular workout but also helps to build strength and endurance. It's like dancing in the pool, where the resistance of the water adds an extra challenge without straining your joints.

Chair exercises are also an excellent choice for those with limited mobility. They offer a chance to engage in strength-building activities from the comfort of a seated position. These exercises can be as simple as arm lifts or leg extensions, focusing on maintaining strength and flexibility in a safe and manageable way. Chair exercises are particularly beneficial for older adults as they help improve balance and prevent falls.

Consistency is key to reaping the benefits of gentle exercises. A weekly exercise schedule can help establish a routine, making it easier to stay committed and motivated. Whether it's a daily walk, bi-weekly yoga sessions or a weekend swim, having a plan keeps you on track. Joining exercise groups, like a local walking club, can provide accountability and encouragement, turning exercise into a social event that you look forward to.

As you consider starting a new exercise routine, safety should always be a priority. A healthcare provider can offer guidance tailored to your needs and abilities, ensuring you choose safe and practical activities. Investing in comfortable workout gear, from supportive shoes to breathable clothing, can enhance your exercise experience, making it more enjoyable and sustainable.

SOCIAL SPORTS: MOVE WHILE YOU GROOVE

It's a sunny afternoon at the local community center. The air is filled with laughter and pickleball paddles striking the ball. Welcome to the arena of social sport, where physical exercise meets the joy of social interaction.

The benefits of social sports extend far beyond the court or field. Whether you're part of a community sports league or organizing informal games with friends, regular play in these activities can significantly improve cardiovascular health and keep your heart healthy. It's a way to move, groove, and laugh to a stronger heart. But it's not just about the physical perks. Social sports also strengthen community bonds, creating a network of friends and acquaintances who rally around a shared interest. The post-game conversations and collective cheer make social sports a delightful blend of exercise and socializing.

Let's take a closer look at some popular social sports. Pickleball, for example, has been growing in popularity. It's a mix of tennis, badminton and ping-pong, played on a smaller court with a paddle and plastic ball. Easy to learn and highly addictive, pickleball offers a full-body workout that's gentle on the joints. It's a sport that turns parks and recreation centers into vibrant hubs of activity and laughter.

Then there's bocce, a low-impact outdoor game perfect for those who enjoy a slower-paced activity. Played on a flat surface, the goal is to roll balls closer to a target ball than your opponents. It's a game of strategy and precision, offering a relaxing yet engaging way to spend an afternoon.

Getting involved in social sports is easier than you might think. Start by exploring local clubs or meetups that cater to your interests. Many communities offer pickleball courts and bocce lanes, with clubs eager to welcome new members. If you're feeling adventurous, consider hosting a neighborhood sports day, where friends and family can gather for a friendly competition. Bring snacks, set up a few games and let the fun unfold. These gatherings bring people together, foster friendships and create memories. So grab a paddle, a ball or whatever equipment you need, and dive in.

EATING WELL FOR LONGEVITY

Nutrition plays a pivotal role in supporting longevity and overall well-being, leading to a healthy and vibrant life in retirement. A nutrient-rich diet is like a well-oiled machine, keeping your body's functions running smoothly while ensuring you have the energy to enjoy each day.

Staying hydrated is the unsung hero of this equation, helping you maintain skin elasticity, joint lubrication, and even cognitive function. So, as you sip that refreshing glass of water, remember: it's doing wonders for your body and mind.

As you explore the world of nutrition, it's essential to focus on key dietary principles that support healthy aging. Incorporating plenty of fruits and vegetables into your diet is one of them, as they provide essential vitamins and minerals that bolster your immune system and keep you feeling your best. Whole grains are another vital component, offering a steady release of energy and keeping your digestive system happy. Lean proteins, whether plant-based or animal-sourced, are building blocks for muscle maintenance and repair. Imagine a colorful salad with grilled chicken or a hearty bowl of quinoa and roasted veggies. These meals satisfy your taste buds and provide the nourishment your body craves.

Meal planning is your ally in maintaining a balanced diet. Create a weekly meal plan that guides you through the week with ease. Such a plan ensures you have all the ingredients you need to whip up delicious and nutritious meals without the stress of last-minute decisions. Cooking in batches can be a lifesaver, providing convenient, ready-to-eat options that save time and effort. You will open the fridge to find a neatly stacked array of pre-prepared, nutritious meals. It's like having a personal chef, all thanks to some planning.

Adapting dietary habits to suit changing nutritional needs is a natural part of aging. Reducing sodium and sugar intake can help maintain healthy blood pressure and reduce the risk of chronic diseases. Explore plant-based meal options, which can surprise you with their unique flavors and textures. A creamy, coconut-based curry, a zesty bean salad or a hearty veggie burger... wholesome meals like these ensure your diet evolves to meet your body's needs while keeping your meals satisfying.

ART OF MINDFUL LIVING

As retirement unfolds, it's an excellent time to prioritize strengthening your body through meditation and mindful living. Adding physical wellness to your bucket list can transform your daily routines. Mindful practices, such as walking meditation or Pilates, help enhance body awareness while promoting physical health. This harmonious blend of mindfulness and movement can improve strength, flexibility and posture while fostering inner peace.

Breathing exercises are a fantastic starting point. They're like a mini-vacation for your mind, where each breath in and out is a step away from the hustle and bustle of daily life. Just a few minutes of focused breathing can lower your heart rate and calm that racing mind, leaving you feeling refreshed and centered.

Guided meditation sessions can take this sense of calm to a whole new level. These sessions offer a structured approach to meditation, making it accessible even to those new to the practice. With the help of an experienced practitioner or teacher verbally guiding you, you are gently led through the process. As you follow along, the teacher prompts you to let go of stress and anxiety, encouraging a deep sense of relaxation and mindfulness as you visualize peaceful landscapes and connect with your breath. Guided meditation with the support of a knowledgeable instructor can enhance mental clarity and nurture emotional well-being, leading to a more balanced and fulfilling life.

Mindfulness meditation is another practice worth exploring. It focuses on present-moment awareness, where you tune into your senses and surroundings without judgment. You might start to notice the sun's warmth on your skin, birds chirping, or the sensation of your feet on the ground. Loving-kindness meditation adds a layer of compassion as you extend goodwill and warmth first to yourself and then to others. It's like sending little waves of kindness out into the world, each returning to you with peace and connection.

Incorporating mindfulness into daily life doesn't have to be complicated. It can be as simple as practicing mindful eating, where you savor each bite, noticing the flavors and textures without distraction. Or it can be a walking meditation in nature, where each step becomes a conscious act that connects you to the earth beneath your feet. These practices inject mindfulness into your daily life, creating moments of calm.

There are plenty of resources at your disposal to deepen your mindfulness practice. Apps like Headspace and Calm offer guided meditations and mindfulness exercises, turning your phone into a pocket-sized meditation coach. Local meditation workshops provide a sense of community and shared experience, allowing you to explore different styles and techniques in a supportive environment. Books and courses on mindfulness can also guide you, offering insights and practices to enrich your journey. Whether you're seeking peace, clarity, or a bit of both, mindfulness and relaxation provide a path for a more centered and harmonious life.

"The measure of your life will not be in what you accumulate, but in what you give away."
— Wayne Dyer

JOY IN SIMPLICITY: DECLUTTER AND RECYCLE

Enter a room free from clutter, where each item tells a story or has a purpose. If you're like me, I often experience a profound sense of peace in such a space, which is a stark contrast to the chaos (and burden) of collecting too many things. Simplify life by letting go of material possessions, and you will experience a greater sense of contentment. It helps you focus on what truly matters—meaningful experiences and cherished memories—not the things that often overwhelm us. When you reduce complexity, you invite tranquility and allow yourself to enjoy life's moments without the distraction of clutter.

Decluttering isn't just about tidying up your home; it's also about freeing yourself from emotional baggage. Letting go of items tied to past emotions can be liberating and creates space for new experiences and growth. A decluttered home offers more than just physical room... it grants mental clarity. It's like opening a window to let fresh air flow through your life, clearing the cobwebs that have settled over time. Blessing others with items you no longer need will lighten your load and bring joy to someone else. Consider donating items to charity, where they can find a new purpose and bring happiness to others. And let's not forget the potential to unlock value by selling possessions and adding a little extra to your savings.

From an environmental perspective, recycling and reusing items can significantly reduce waste and carbon footprint. It's a small step with a significant impact, contributing to a healthier planet. Decluttering with gratitude and mindfulness ensures that your possessions are appreciated for their role in your life before they move on. Approach each item with appreciation, acknowledging its purpose and letting it go with kindness.

The next step is to organize essentials and ensure that what remains is valuable and meaningful. Create a living space that reflects who you are now, not who you were in the past.

My uncle Jeffrey, for one, decided to downsize to a smaller home when he retired in his late 6os. He found that the process of letting go was cathartic and transformative. He and his wife discovered joy in a spacious, uncluttered environment where he could focus on his painting and guitar jamming. He blessed his community by donating items to local charities, finding peace in the knowledge that they would continue to be valued and used. Uncle Jeffrey's story is a testament to the fulfillment of embracing simplicity.

DIGITAL DETOX

In today's hyper-connected world, it's easy to fall into the trap of excessive screen time. We often find ourselves glued to our devices, checking emails, scrolling through social media, or binge-watching the latest TV series. While technology offers countless conveniences, too much screen time can lead to mental fatigue and elevated stress levels. Our brains, constantly bombarded with information, rarely get a chance to rest. This digital overload can disrupt sleep patterns, leaving us tossing and turning instead of enjoying restorative slumber. We wake up feeling more exhausted than refreshed, and the cycle continues. It's like running on a treadmill that never stops.

A digital detox retreat can be a refreshing way to hit the reset button. Such a retreat is more than just a break from screens; it's an opportunity to rediscover the richness of life beyond digital devices.

Start by choosing a serene and tech-free location, perhaps a cabin in the woods or a cozy beach cottage. The key is finding a spot that encourages relaxation and disconnection from the digital frenzy. Once you've chosen your destination, set clear detox goals and intentions. Are you looking to unwind, spark creativity, or enjoy the beauty of the present moment? Defining your purpose helps steer the retreat in a meaningful direction.

Engaging in offline activities is the heart of a digital detox retreat. Instead of reaching for your phone, pick up a book or dive into creative arts like painting or crafting. These activities stimulate your mind and offer a sense of accomplishment and joy. Practicing yoga or meditation can further enhance the experience, grounding you in the present and helping you reconnect with your inner self. Imagine starting your day with a sunrise yoga session or spending an afternoon sketching the landscape. These moments, devoid of digital distractions, invite peace and fulfillment.

Reflecting on the detox experience is an integral part of the process. Take time to journal about the insights and feelings you've gained. What was it like to be free from the constant ping of notifications? How did it feel to engage fully with your surroundings? Writing down these reflections can offer clarity and perspective, helping you understand the impact of digital overload on your well-being. As you return to your daily life, consider how you might incorporate these insights into a more balanced relationship with technology.

NATURE THERAPY

Nature is a great ally when you need help to strengthen your body during retirement. Imagine stepping outside, the morning sun gently warming your face and body. This is nature's therapy at work.

Spending time outdoors is a balm for both the mind and body. Fresh air nourishes your lungs, while natural light boosts your vitamin D levels, supporting bone health and mood regulation. It's Mother Nature's way of giving you a warm hug. Studies have shown that exposure to nature reduces stress levels, calming the mind and soothing the spirit. The rhythmic sounds of rustling leaves or flowing water can relax even the busiest minds, creating a sense of peace that's hard to find indoors.

There are countless ways to enjoy the great outdoors. If you like strolls, consider exploring local hiking trails or nature walks. These outings offer a chance to stretch your legs and immerse yourself in the beauty of diverse landscapes. Bird-watching or wildlife observation can be equally rewarding, offering a glimpse into the fascinating world of nature's creatures. Armed with binoculars, you can transform a simple walk into an adventure, spotting colorful birds or catching a glimpse of deer grazing in the distance. These activities invite you to slow down, observe, and appreciate the wonders of the natural world, fostering a deeper connection with the environment.

Consistent interaction with nature is key to reaping its benefits. Scheduling weekly outdoor outings ensures that you make time for these rejuvenating experiences. Regular exposure to nature can significantly boost your overall well-being, whether it's a weekend hike or a midweek walk in the park. Creating a home garden or green space offers another avenue for enjoying nature daily. Tending to your plants and watching them grow and thrive under your care is one rewarding endeavor. Not only does it bring a piece of the outdoors into your home, but it also offers a sanctuary where you can find solace.

To take your interaction with nature one step further, consider forest bathing. Rooted in the Japanese practice of shinrin-yoku, forest bathing is an invigorating nature therapy that offers participants a holistic way to strengthen their bodies and minds. Immersing ourselves in the tranquility of a forest encourages relaxation and reduces stress, while the natural environment promotes physical activity, from gentle walks to mindful exploration. The fresh air, vibrant foliage and soothing sounds enhance well-being and boost immunity. Regular forest bathing fosters a deeper connection to nature, encouraging overall vitality and rejuvenation.

Safety is paramount when engaging in outdoor activities. Preparing for varying weather conditions ensures that your outings are enjoyable and comfortable. Dressing in layers allows you to adapt to changing temperatures, while a hat and sunscreen can protect you from the sun's harmful rays. Practice Leave No Trace principles to respect and preserve the natural environment for future generations.

The great outdoors offers more than just a pretty view. It's a source of healing and renewal. Whether hiking a trail, watching a bird, or tending to your garden, these moments invite you to breathe deeply, live fully, and find peace in the world. If your retirement goal is to strengthen your body, regular interaction with nature can significantly enhance your health and wellness.

MAKE AN IMPACT WITH YOUR REVIEW

*"Service to others is the rent you pay for
your room here on Earth."*

MUHAMMAD ALI

When you share your experiences, you light the way for someone else. Let's spark that light together.

Have you ever felt unsure about what to do with your time in retirement? You're not alone! Many people are excited but also curious about how to make the most of this special time in their lives.

My goal is to help everyone enjoy a retirement that's engaging, colorful and filled with purpose.

But to spread the joy and reach more people, I need your help.

Most folks pick books based on what others say about them. That's why I'm asking you to take a moment to write a review. Your thoughts could guide a retiree or someone getting ready to retire toward the adventure of a lifetime.

It's quick and easy—just a minute of your time. Your review could help…

- one more traveler embark on a new journey.
- one more hobbyist explore their creative side.
- one more neighbor give back to the community.
- one more friend find a new passion.
- one more person discover their retirement dreams.

To help make a difference, just scan the below QR code and share your review:

If you enjoy lifting others up, then you're the perfect person to share your thoughts. Thank you so much for being part of this exciting journey.

Warm wishes,
Eliza Golding

CHAPTER 6
E: ELEVATE THE SOUL

"Adventure isn't just for the young; it's for the young at heart." These words by Eileen, a 55-year-old from Singapore, remind us that the thrill of discovery doesn't have an expiry date. Upon retiring, Eileen turned her love for sketching into an epic adventure, traveling across Europe with her husband, a backpack and a sketchpad. She captured the essence of bustling markets in Paris, serene canals in Venice, and the rolling vineyards of Tuscany. Each stroke of her pencil was a record of life's beauty. Eileen's inspiring life choice shows we don't have to slow down upon retirement. On the contrary, we can find new rhythms that uplift the soul.

Welcome to the last element of the W.I.S.E. bucket list. If you seek experiences that speak to your spirit and fill you with wonder and awe when you retire, this chapter is for you. Purpose-driven adventures are the core of 'Elevate the Soul', and your ticket to an unforgettable retirement. Align your activities with your heart's desires and create experiences that enrich your life and inspire those around you. It could be a hiking trip through the Appalachian Trail or a serene retreat by the sea... each adventure is an invitation to explore the world and yourself.

Creative hobbies, too, offer a canvas for self-expression and exploration. Rediscover the joy of creating, whether it's through painting, writing or crafting, bringing joy to your everyday life. These hobbies are a way to connect with your innermost self and to express emotions and ideas that words alone cannot capture. Picture yourself in a pottery class, your hands shaping clay into something beautiful and unique. This act of creation reminds you of the magic within you, waiting to be shared with the world.

Reflections

Take a moment to reflect on what elevates your soul. Is it the thrill of adventure, the joy of creation, or the wonder of travel? Consider creating a vision board or journal to capture your dreams and aspirations.

What activities or experiences call to you? How can you incorporate them into your retirement? Use this reflection to guide your journey, ensuring each step aligns with your passions and purpose.

Of course, no bucket list is complete without travel. You could be standing at the edge of the Grand Canyon, the vastness of the landscape stretching out before you. This moment of awe is a reminder of the world's wonders and your place within it. Or you could be in Japan during cherry blossom season, basking amongst the pink blooms that symbolize renewal and beauty. These experiences are not just about the destinations; they are opportunities to step outside your comfort zone, engage with different cultures and perspectives, and create memories that enrich your soul.

DISCOVERING LOCAL HIDDEN GEMS

Many of us take for granted the interesting places and experiences that exist within our own backyard. Retirement is the perfect time to unravel or rediscover these hidden gems and lesser-known attractions. They could be local museums and historical sites that offer a window into the past, revealing stories that have shaped your community. They could also be parks and nature reserves, where you can lose yourself in their tranquil beauty. These local wonders provide a sense of adventure without needing distant travel, transforming the familiar into the extraordinary.

Community events and festivals are worth exploring, as they are vibrant celebrations of local culture. Farmers' markets and craft fairs burst with colors, flavors and the creativity of local artisans. Experience the joy of tasting fresh produce, chatting with vendors, and discovering unique handmade treasures. Then there are local music and arts festivals that offer a stage for talent and creativity, where every note and brushstroke tells a story. These events enrich your life with new experiences and foster a sense of belonging and connection with your community. They're a delightful way to explore new interests and support local artists and businesses.

Local travel offers the charm of adventure with the convenience of proximity. Reduced travel costs and the chance to support your local economy make nearby adventures attractive. Use public transportation or hop on a bike to explore your surroundings, reducing your carbon footprint while enjoying the journey. Dining at local, family-owned restaurants introduces you to the culinary delights of your region. Each bite is a taste of home, infused with the stories and traditions of the people who crafted it. These small journeys invite you to see your community with fresh eyes and a renewed appreciation.

Uncovering local secrets is like a treasure hunt, where each hidden gem adds a new layer to your understanding of your community. Joining local social media groups can provide insider tips and recommendations that lead you to unexpected discoveries. These platforms are like maps that guide you to the uncharted territories of your neighborhood. Ask friends and neighbors for their favorite spots; their insights may lead you to a charming café or a secluded park you never knew existed. Explore the familiar in new ways, and celebrate the community that surrounds you.

ROAD TRIPS AND RV'ING

Road trips and RV travel offer the freedom to explore at your own pace, where each journey is filled with endless possibilities. There's no rush, no rigid schedules—just you, the open road, and a playlist of your favorite tunes. Cruise along scenic highways and stop whenever curiosity strikes... this could be in the form of a charming roadside diner, or a quirky museum. These trips allow for spontaneity, the kind that can lead to unexpected encounters and stories worth telling.

Planning a successful road trip requires a bit of forethought, but it doesn't have to be daunting. Start with a playlist that captures the spirit of adventure, turning every mile into a memorable moment. Pack essentials like snacks, water and a trusty first-aid kit to keep you fueled and prepared. Safety is crucial, so ensure your vehicle is road-ready with routine checks. Consider the weather and road conditions, adjusting your plans as needed. Whether charting a course or letting the road guide you, the beauty lies in the journey and the freedom to explore.

RV travel takes the road trip experience to a whole new level. It offers the comforts of home while you venture into the unknown. With an RV, remote locations and stunning natural settings are within reach, providing a front-row seat to the world's wonders. Choosing the right RV size and type is crucial for comfort and ease. Consider your needs and preferences, ensuring you have the most essential amenities. Don't forget to reserve campsites or RV parks in advance, as this can save you from last-minute scrambles, allowing you to focus on the joy of exploration.

VOLUNTOURISM: GIVING BACK WHILE SEEING THE WORLD

Do you know you can wake up to birds singing in a lush forest, knowing you'll help preserve this natural wonder today? Yes, this is possible with voluntourism, which merges the joy of travel with the satisfaction of making a difference. You might participate in environmental conservation projects, like planting trees to combat deforestation or assisting in wildlife protection. Or you might venture into rural communities, teaching English and opening doors to new opportunities for young learners. These experiences don't just enrich the lives of those you help. They also offer you a deeper cultural understanding and a sense of purpose.

Choosing the right voluntourism opportunity is essential. You'll want to ensure that your efforts genuinely benefit host communities. Start by researching organizations thoroughly. Look for those with strong track records and positive reviews from past volunteers. The projects must align with your values and skills. Whether you're passionate about education, conservation or humanitarianism, there's a program out there that needs your unique talents. Aligning your skills with the community's needs ensures that your contribution is meaningful and effective.

Numerous platforms can connect you with reputable voluntourism opportunities. Organizations like WWOOF (World Wide Opportunities on Organic Farms) and the Peace Corps are well-known for their ethical practices and impactful programs. Websites specializing in ethical travel can also help you find the right fit. Reading testimonials from previous volunteers can provide insights into what to expect and help you avoid potential pitfalls. Their stories often highlight the profound impact of their experiences, both on themselves and the communities they served. Host communities frequently express gratitude, sharing how these collaborations have fostered growth and development. So, pack your bags, bring your skills, and prepare to make a difference while exploring the world.

VIRTUAL TRAVEL: EXPLORING THE WORLD FROM HOME

Sip your favorite cup of tea while strolling through the corridors of the Louvre or exploring the ancient ruins of Machu Picchu—all from the comfort of your living room! Virtual travel offers retirees the chance to experience global destinations without the hassle of packing a suitcase or enduring long flights. You can wander through museums and landmarks with virtual tours, soaking in art and history at your own pace. Online cultural experiences bring the world to your doorstep, offering everything from live theater performances to culinary classes, accessible with just a click.

Virtual reality (VR) and augmented reality (AR) are game-changers in digital exploration. VR platforms provide immersive experiences, transporting you to distant lands with stunning realism. Don a headset and suddenly you're standing in the bustling streets of Tokyo or the serene landscapes of Iceland. Meanwhile, AR apps can enhance local adventures by overlaying historical insights and interactive elements onto real-world locations. These technologies offer travel experiences that allow you to explore without boundaries.

To make the most of virtual travel, platforms like Google Arts & Culture offer extensive museum tours and cultural insights. Many other websites provide online travel experiences that offer unique glimpses into different parts of the world. Engaging with travel enthusiasts through digital platforms can enrich your experiences even further. These include social media groups and online forums, which are gathering places for sharing stories, tips and even travelogues. Participating in webinars and podcasts connects you with like-minded adventurers, allowing you to learn, share and dream.

Tips for Virtual Trips

Here're some websites offering unique online travel experiences. Immersive videos, interactive virtual tours, live-stream events... the world is just a click away:

• **Wander**: Explore global destinations via Google Maps in a virtual format. Visit: https://wandermaps.com/

• **AirPano**: This site offers 360-degree aerial panoramas of global locations. Visit: https://www.airpano.com/

• **Google Arts & Culture**: Explore museums and art collections with virtual tours and interactive exhibits. Visit: https://artsandculture.google.com/

MUSEUM HOPPING FOR ART AND HISTORY

Wander through the grand halls of the Louvre, stand before the Mona Lisa's enigmatic smile, or marvel at The Met's (Metropolitan Museum of Art) vast collection of art from around the globe. Museums like these transport you to different eras, offering a glimpse into humanity's rich culture and history. Whether you're exploring ancient Egypt's wonders or modern art's avant-garde movements, each visit is a passport to another world. Don't overlook regional museums either, as they hold local history treasures, telling stories of their communities. These smaller venues often provide intimate experiences, connecting you deeply with the place you call home.

Museum memberships are a smart way to enrich these experiences without breaking the bank. They offer year-round access, allowing you to explore at your leisure. Many memberships come with perks like exclusive openings or lectures, giving you behind-the-curtain peeks at how exhibits come together. Plus, there's something special about being part of a museum community, knowing you support the arts and contribute to cultural preservation.

Consider joining guided tours or using audio guides to maximize your museum visits. These resources bring exhibits to life, offering insights that might go unnoticed. Workshops and special events enhance your understanding, providing hands-on opportunities to engage with art and history.

Documenting your visits adds a personal touch to the experience. Keep a travel journal or sketchbook to capture your thoughts and impressions. Photography, too, offers a way to preserve your favorite moments, but remember to respect museum rules. Whether it's a close-up of a painting's texture or a candid shot of a friend in deep contemplation, these snapshots become cherished memories of your artistic explorations.

CULTURAL FESTIVALS: A WORLD OF EXPERIENCES

Cultural festivals are portals into the heart of different societies, offering immersive experiences that showcase the richness of global traditions. From the dazzling array of films at international cinema festivals to the heartfelt celebrations at local heritage events, each festival invites you to step into a story more significant than your own. These gatherings are more than just spectacles. They are celebrations of diversity. Attending a film festival might mean seeing the world through a director's lens. Meanwhile, a local heritage festival could immerse you in the customs of a community that may be just around the corner or halfway across the globe.

Finding and attending these cultural gems requires curiosity and detective work. Local cultural centers often have calendars brimming with programs, and travel guides can be your best friend when seeking international festivals. Websites dedicated to cultural events are also treasure troves of information. They can guide you to the best times and places, helping you plan trips that align with your interests.

When participating in festivals, don't just observe, but engage too. Workshops and demonstrations are often part of the festivities, offering hands-on learning that deepens your understanding and appreciation of cultures different from yours. These interactions can be eye-opening, fostering connections with people from diverse backgrounds. You might find yourself learning a traditional dance or trying your hand at a local craft, each moment a chance to grow and connect.

For those who seek deeper involvement, volunteering at festivals offers a backstage pass to the action. Helping out at events gives you insights into the inner workings, from setting up stages to coordinating performers. This behind-the-scenes access enriches your experience, providing a sense of contribution and belonging. Participating in cultural dance or music performances can further deepen your involvement. You don't have to be a professional; an open heart and willingness to join in are often all that's required. Such experiences bring you closer to the essence of the festival, turning passive observation into active participation.

TRAVEL ON A SHOESTRING

Traveling on a budget might seem daunting, but with creativity and savvy planning, it's possible to explore the world without emptying your wallet. One of the best-kept secrets in budget travel is the off-peak discount. Traveling during the off-season saves money on flights and accommodation and means fewer crowds and a more relaxed experience. Stroll through the streets of Rome without the usual hustle and bustle, or enjoy a quiet beach in Thailand when the peak-season tourists have long gone. Budget airlines are another fantastic option. They might not offer the frills of first-class travel, but they get you from point A to point B without breaking the bank. Pair this with affordable accommodations, like hostels or budget hotels, and you're on your way to an adventure that doesn't cost the earth.

Creating a cost-effective itinerary is all about balancing free attractions with paid experiences. Many cities offer free walking tours or have museums with free entry days. Take advantage of local transportation, like buses or subways, to explore your surroundings affordably.

Travel hacking is another handy tool for the budget-conscious traveler. Reward points and travel credit cards can earn free flights or hotel stays, making those dream destinations more accessible. Consider house-sitting or home exchange programs, which allow you to stay in comfortable homes without the hotel price tag. Websites like Meetup can help you find local events or activities, often at a fraction of the cost or even for free. Others like The Points Guy, Nomadic Matt, Travel Freely, Next Vacay, Airfarewatchdog, just to name a few, share resources on budget travel, provide tools for finding flight deals, and offer tips on maximizing credit card rewards and tracking loyalty programs. Apps offering discounts on attractions can also stretch your budget further, ensuring you get the most out of your journey without skimping on the experience.

BLENDING TECH AND TRAVEL THROUGH DIGITAL NOMADING

The digital nomad lifestyle offers a unique blend of freedom and flexibility, allowing you to work remotely while exploring new locales. This lifestyle opens the door to new cultures and cuisines, allowing you to immerse in local traditions. It's the perfect way to live a life less ordinary, where work and travel coexist harmoniously. You can choose where you want to live, whether it's a bustling city in Southeast Asia or a quiet coastal town in Europe. Each place brings new adventures, both professionally and personally.

Cities known for their tech-friendly environments, like Lisbon, Berlin, Austin, Stockholm, Singapore and Chiang Mai, have become havens for digital nomads. These places offer affordable living and coworking spaces, making it easier to balance work and leisure. You'll find communities of like-minded individuals eager to network and share experiences. Digital tools and apps like Upwork and Slack connect you with employers and clients, ensuring you can maintain productivity while on the move. It's the best of both worlds, allowing you to earn a living while exploring the world. You can work in the morning and spend your afternoons at local markets or beautiful beaches.

My friend Isaac was once an art director confined to a dreary office space. At age 50, with an earnest desire for change, he decided to trade his cubicle for a life of adventure. He packed his bags, took his skills on the road, and hasn't looked back. Embracing the digital nomad lifestyle with open arms, he had transformed his work life into a journey of discovery.

From designing logos amidst the lush landscapes of Bali to creating websites against a backdrop of historic sites in Mexico, he found a way to fuse his passion for travel with his career.

Isaac's story is a testament to the seamless integration of work and wanderlust. His experience highlights the opportunities the digital nomad lifestyle affords for pre- and semi-retirees, marrying his career aspirations with his love for travel. With digital nomading, you don't just escape the nine-to-five grind. You create a lifestyle that aligns with your values and dreams. You get a chance to redefine what work means to you, all while collecting memories from every corner of the globe.

CREATIVE HOBBIES: LOW-COST AND ENRICHING

Exploring affordable hobbies is like opening a treasure chest of possibilities. You don't need to spend a fortune to find joy and fulfillment. Take gardening, for example. You can start with recycled materials, like using old containers as planters, or collecting seeds from fruits you already consume. This eco-friendly approach not only saves money but also encourages creativity. Plus, there's something gratifying about watching a tiny seed grow into a flourishing plant.

Similarly, photography doesn't require an expensive camera. Your smartphone can capture stunning images of everyday moments. With an eye for detail and a bit of experimentation, you can create beautiful snapshots of life's little wonders.

Joining hobby groups can add a social dimension to your interests. Community art classes or clubs provide a shared space where you can learn from others, exchange ideas, and perhaps even collaborate on projects.

DIY projects are a perfect way to express creativity without breaking the bank. Making homemade candles or soap can be fun and functional, allowing you to experiment with scents and colors. Upcycling old furniture into new pieces breathes life into forgotten items, transforming them into unique treasures. These projects beautify your living space and provide a sense of accomplishment. The beauty of DIY lies in its simplicity—you don't need fancy tools or extensive skills, just a willingness to try and a little imagination.

Free or low-cost resources can further enhance your hobby experience. The internet is a goldmine of free tutorials and courses that can guide you through almost any project you can imagine. Whether it's knitting, painting or learning a new instrument, there's likely a video or article out there to help you get started. Local libraries are another fantastic resource, often lending out materials or tools you might need. By tapping into these resources, you can expand your skills and explore new interests without spending a dime. This approach saves money and opens doors to a world of creative possibilities.

CULINARY ADVENTURES

Food is a universal language, a gateway to understanding cultures and traditions. Exploring ethnic cuisines at local restaurants can transport you to far-off lands without leaving your neighborhood. You can savor the complex spices of Indian cuisine one day and then dive into the delicate flavors of Japanese sushi the next. Each dish tells a story, offering a taste of the culture from which it hails.

Attending international food festivals is like taking a culinary tour around the world. These gatherings invite you to sample diverse flavors, each bite an adventure in itself. But why stop at a tasting when you can create? Cooking classes focusing on global cuisines open a window into the world's kitchens. With them, you can master the art of French pastry, roll out dough with the precision of a seasoned chef, or learn the secrets of Italian pasta making. Discovering the spices and ingredients of different regions enhances your cooking skills and deepens your appreciation of the culinary arts.

Culinary travel takes this exploration further, offering unique insights into cultural traditions through food. Planning trips centered around gastronomy allows you to immerse yourself in the essence of a place. You could be wandering through Marrakech's bustling markets or visiting a culinary school in Tuscany to learn authentic Italian cooking.

Back home, consider hosting cultural culinary events to share your culinary discoveries with others. You could organize an international potluck, where friends bring dishes from different cultures, or you could host a themed dinner party with recipes and cooking techniques from your travels. Sharing these experiences enriches your culinary repertoire and fosters connections with those around you.

LITERATURE AND FILM: STORIES FROM AROUND THE GLOBE

Literature and film hold the keys to worlds beyond our own, offering glimpses into cultures, values and lives that differ from ours. A novel by Gabriel García Márquez, for instance, will transport you into the magical realism of Latin America. These stories, translated from their native languages, provide windows into the soul of a culture, revealing its joys, struggles and dreams. Similarly, watching foreign films or documentaries can transport you to distant lands, allowing you to experience the sights, sounds and emotions of a place without leaving your couch. A French film may capture the romance of Parisian life, while a Japanese documentary might reveal the tranquility of a tea ceremony, each frame a lesson in cultural understanding.

Selecting diverse reading materials is like embarking on a literary treasure hunt. Start by exploring works by Nobel Prize-winning authors whose stories have been celebrated for their depth and universality. Delve into contemporary world literature, where modern voices offer fresh perspectives on timeless themes. Each book becomes a passport, taking you on journeys through time and space.

Film festivals are another avenue for cultural immersion, showcasing international cinema that tells stories from around the globe. You can attend renowned events like the Cannes Film Festival or the Sundance Film Festival, or explore local film festivals with diverse lineups. These gatherings celebrate the art of storytelling and the diversity of human experience.

Discussing and sharing these cultural stories can enrich your understanding even further. Joining a book club with an international focus opens the door to lively conversations and differing viewpoints. Imagine debating the themes of a Russian novel or dissecting the symbolism in a Korean film; each discussion is an opportunity to learn and grow. Hosting film nights with friends can spark thought-provoking talks, where each movie becomes a catalyst for conversation. Through literature and film, you engage with the world in all its complexity and beauty.

Legendary Reads: Nobel Literature Prize-Winners

The Nobel Prize in Literature honors authors who have produced exceptional work reflecting the human experience, showcasing the power of words to inspire & provoke thought. Here are some of these authors and their notable works:

- **Ernest Hemingway (1954)** – Acclaimed for his impactful prose in iconic works like *The Old Man and the Sea* and *A Farewell to Arms.*

- **Alice Munro (2013)** – Awarded for her mastery of the short story, such as *Dear Life* and *Dance of the Happy Shades.*

- **Kazuo Ishiguro (2017)** – Awarded for his exceptional narrative artistry, in works such as *Never Let Me Go* and *The Remains of the Day.*

- **Toni Morrison (1993)** – Honored for her visionary literature including *Beloved,* which explores African American identity.

- **Doris Lessing (2007)** – Awarded for her deep understanding of social dynamics in *The Golden Notebook* and *The Grass is Singing.*

- **John Steinbeck (1962)** – Renowned for his exploration of social issues in *The Grapes of Wrath* and *East of Eden.*

- **Gabriel García Márquez (1982)** – Celebrated for his masterful storytelling in works like *One Hundred Years of Solitude* and *Love in the Time of Cholera.*

- **Jean-Marie Gustave Le Clézio (2008)** – Honored for his poetic exploration of humanity in novels like *Desert* and *The African.*

DANCE, MUSIC, RHYTHMS AND MOVEMENTS

There's something magical about losing yourself in the rhythm of a dance or the melody of a song. Dance and music are universal languages that speak to the heart and soul, reflecting people's cultural identity and history worldwide. Experience the thrill of attending live performances where traditional dances come alive, each step telling a story passed down through generations. Whether it's the fiery passion of flamenco in Spain or the graceful movements of ballet in Russia, these art forms showcase the beauty and diversity of global cultures. Each performance is a window into the traditions and values that have shaped communities, offering a glimpse into their unique heritage.

But why watch when you can join in the fun? Dance classes like salsa or tango invite you to become part of the rhythm, feel the music in your bones and express yourself through movement. These classes aren't just for the young but for anyone who wants to embrace life with open arms. Perhaps learning to play a musical instrument from another culture piques your interest. Whether strumming a guitar or tapping on bongos, music lessons open doors to new worlds of sound and creativity.

Festivals are another excellent way to experience dance and music. Picture yourself surrounded by vibrant costumes and infectious beats at a local cultural festival or parade. These events create a lively atmosphere, inviting everyone to participate and celebrate. You can travel to international festivals like Carnival in Brazil or Oktoberfest in Germany, where music and dance are at the heart of the festivities. These gatherings bring people together, fostering connections and understanding. The energy and excitement of festival participation linger long after the last note has been played, leaving you with cherished memories and newfound friends.

Creating a personal cultural playlist can transport you to different worlds without leaving your home. Curate a music collection from global artists on streaming platforms, exploring genres that pique your curiosity. Attend virtual concerts or music events to experience live performances from the comfort of your living room. These musical journeys offer a rich universe of sounds and stories, inviting you to explore the rhythms and melodies of cultures far and wide.

EPIC VACATIONS: ICONIC TRAVEL DESTINATIONS ACROSS THE WORLD

Retirement opens the door to incredible travel adventures, offering you THE opportunity to embark on vacations across the globe. Although this book is not solely about travel, the latter makes a big difference to a life well lived, and the book will be incomplete without it. Therefore I'm dedicating this section to vacation ideas that will enrich your retirement life.

Already have a travel bucket list that's bursting at its seams? Clueless as to where to start? Here are some of my recommendations to bolster, re-model or jumpstart your list. Curated with your retirement priorities and needs in mind, my suggestions focus on leisurely, purpose-driven exploration and provide insights to help you maximize your travel experiences without breaking the bank.

Explore breathtaking landscapes. Stroll through vibrant cities. Encounter remarkable landmarks. Each adventure promises excitement as well as an opportunity to deepen your understanding of the world and its rich history and culture.

TOP 8 UNESCO WORLD HERITAGE SITES

Let's start with the crème de la crème of travel destinations: the UNESCO World Heritage Sites. These are places so significant that they've been recognized by UNESCO (the United Nations Educational, Scientific and Cultural Organization) for their outstanding cultural or natural significance that showcases the planet's diversity and heritage. They are landmarks or areas with legal protection by international treaties. Each site blends history, culture and natural beauty and offers awe-inspiring activities.

The Pyramids of Giza, Egypt

These iconic structures are the last of the Seven Wonders of the Ancient World, showcasing the grandeur of ancient Egyptian civilization.

Main attraction: The Great Pyramid of Khufu, the largest of the three pyramids and a must-see.

Must-do activities: Take a guided tour to discover the history of the pyramids and enjoy a camel ride around the Giza Plateau.

Tips: Visit during the cooler months (October to April) and consider a twilight tour for a magical experience. Look for group tours to save on expenses.

The Great Wall of China, China

A marvel of human ingenuity, this ancient fortification stretches over 13,000 miles and represents centuries of history.

Main attractions: Several well-preserved and easily accessible sections, such as Badaling and Mutianyu.

Must-do activities: Walk along the wall, take a cable car for stunning views, and visit nearby watchtowers.

Tips: Visit in the spring or fall for pleasant weather and fewer crowds. Use public transportation to reach the wall and save on costs.

Machu Picchu, Peru

Often referred to as the "Lost City of the Incas", Machu Picchu is a stunning symbol of the Inca Empire, showcasing extraordinary architectural prowess and engineering.

Main attraction: The ancient ruins, which house intricate stone structures, terraces and stunning panoramic views of the surrounding Andes Mountains.

Must-do activities: Take the scenic train from Cusco to Aguas Calientes, stroll through the archaeological site, and enjoy a guided tour to learn about Inca history.

Tips: The best time to visit is during the dry season, which runs from May to September. Avoid peak hours by going early in the morning or late afternoon.

The Colosseum, Italy

This ancient amphitheater is a testament to Roman architecture and engineering and a symbol of Italy's rich history.

Main attraction: The Colosseum, with its impressive arches and tiered seating, which used to host monumental events like gladiator games.

Must-do activities: Join a guided tour to skip the lines and explore the underground chambers and arena floor.

Tips: The best time to visit for milder weather is spring (April to June) or early fall (September to October). Opt for evening visits to avoid the day crowds.

Acropolis of Athens, Greece

The Acropolis is an enduring symbol of Ancient Greece and democracy. It houses several significant buildings, including the Parthenon.

Main attraction: The Parthenon, which is dedicated to the goddess Athena.

Must-do activities: Explore the Acropolis Museum and stroll around the archaeological site.

Tips: The best time to visit is late spring or early fall to avoid the heat. For value, use a combined ticket to access other historical sites in Athens.

The Historic Center of Florence, Italy

Renowned for its art and architecture, Florence is the birthplace of the Renaissance.

Main attractions: The stunning Duomo and the Uffizi Galleries, filled with masterpieces.

Must-do activities: Stroll through the Boboli Gardens, admire Michelangelo's David, and take in the views from Piazzale Michelangelo.

Tips: Visit during spring or fall for an enjoyable experience with fewer tourists. Make museum reservations online to avoid long lines.

Djenne, Mali

Djenne is famous for its unique mud architecture, particularly the Great Mosque, which represents the Sudano-Sahelian style. It highlights the city's historical role as an African trade and culture center.

Main attraction: The Great Mosque, an architectural marvel and one of the most extensive mud buildings in the world.

Must-do activities: Check out the market day, explore local artisan shops, and take guided tours of the mosque and surrounding area to learn about Djenne's history and culture.

Tips: The best time to visit is between November and February when the weather is cooler. To save on costs, consider staying in local guesthouses. Enjoy street food, which can provide an authentic taste of the culture and save on dining expenses.

Teotihuacan, Mexico

Teotihuacan, meaning "City of the Gods", is an ancient Mesoamerican city known for its architectural wonders and historical importance. It was one of the largest cities in the ancient world and is a significant archaeological site.

Main attractions: The Pyramid of the Sun and the Pyramid of the Moon – the primary highlights of this ancient city.

Must-do activities: Climb the Pyramid of the Sun for panoramic views, stroll along the Avenue of the Dead, and explore the various temples and murals to learn about Teotihuacan's fascinating history.

Tips: The ideal time to visit is during the dry season, from November to April. To save on admission fees, arrive early in the day to take advantage of fewer crowds, and look for guided group tours that can provide valuable insights at a lower cost.

TOP 6 ICONIC NATURAL LANDSCAPES

Exploring iconic natural landscapes is an excellent way for retirees to connect with nature while enjoying breathtaking views and unique experiences. Here are six stunning destinations worldwide.

Banff National Park, Canada

Nestled in the Canadian Rockies, Banff National Park is Canada's oldest national park. It is renowned for its stunning mountain scenery and abundant wildlife.

Main attraction: The spectacular turquoise waters of Lake Louise, surrounded by towering peaks.

Must-do activities: Take a leisurely walk along the lakeshore, explore the scenic drive to Moraine Lake, and ride the Banff Gondola for breathtaking views.

Tips: The best time to visit is from June to September when the weather is warm and trails are accessible. To save on costs, consider staying in nearby towns like Canmore, where accommodations can be more affordable.

Mount Fuji, Japan

Mount Fuji is Japan's tallest peak and a symbol of national identity, attracting visitors to its stunning beauty and cultural significance.

Main attraction: The breathtaking view of Mount Fuji, especially from nearby lakes like Lake Kawaguchi.

Must-do activities: Consider a relaxing boat ride on Lake Kawaguchi or enjoy a peaceful walk around the area. Visit the Fuji Five Lakes (Fujigoko) region for picturesque views.

Tips: For beautiful scenery, the best time to visit is during the cherry blossom season (April) or autumn (October to November). I strongly recommend using Japan's efficient public transportation system to reduce travel costs.

Victoria Falls, Zambia/Zimbabwe

One of the world's largest and most famous waterfalls, Victoria Falls is known as Mosi-oa-Tunya, or "The Smoke That Thunders".

Main attraction: The expansive water curtain plunging 108 meters, creating a breathtaking spectacle.

Must-do activities: Take a guided walking tour of the falls, enjoy a sunset cruise on the Zambezi River, or visit nearby national parks for wildlife viewing.

Tips: The best time to visit is from February to May, after the rainy season when the falls are at their fullest. Consider visiting during the shoulder seasons to avoid large crowds and find better deals on accommodations.

Santorini, Greece

Santorini is famous for its stunning volcanic landscapes, whitewashed buildings, and crystal-clear waters, making it one of the most picturesque islands in the Aegean Sea.

Main attractions: The iconic caldera views and spectacular sunsets from the coastal town of Oia.

Must-do activities: Enjoy strolls through the charming streets of Fira and Oia, relax on unique beaches like Red Beach and Kamari, and consider a wine-tasting tour to sample local varieties.

Tips: The best time to visit is in late spring (April to June) or early fall (September to October) for mild weather and fewer tourists. To save money, consider visiting during the shoulder seasons or booking accommodations away from the main tourist areas.

Lake Bled, Slovenia

Lake Bled is a stunning glacial lake known for its picturesque scenery, complete with an island with a charming church and a medieval castle perched on a hill.

Main attraction: The postcard-perfect view of Bled Castle overlooking the lake.

Must-do activities: Rent a traditional Pletna boat to visit Bled Island, hike to Bled Castle for spectacular panoramic views, and try the famous local cream cake (kremna rezina).

Tips: The best times to visit are late spring (May to June) and early fall (September to October) for pleasant weather and vibrant colors. To save money, look for local guesthouses or rentals instead of hotels and enjoy exploring the area on foot.

Zhangjiajie National Forest Park, China

Zhangjiajie National Forest Park is famous for its towering sandstone pillars, which inspired the floating mountains in the movie Avatar. It showcases stunning geological formations and diverse ecosystems, making it a unique natural wonder.

Main attraction: The thousands of sandstone pillars which reach heights of up to 1,000 meters, creating a surreal landscape with breathtaking views.

Must-do activities: Take a stroll on the Zhangjiajie Glass Bridge for an adrenaline rush as you walk across the world's longest and highest glass bridge, offering stunning views. Don't miss the cable car ride to Tianmen Mountain for panoramic vistas and visit the famous Taoist Temple atop the mountain.

Tips: The best time to visit is spring (April to June) or autumn (September to November) when the weather is comfortable and the landscape shows vibrant colors. To save time, consider purchasing a multi-day pass, which allows you to explore at a relaxed pace. Early mornings are great for avoiding the larger tour groups and enjoying the park with fewer crowds.

TOP 8 VIBRANT CITIES

If you are like me, who love the sights and sounds of lively urban environments, here are eight vibrant cities around the globe that offer rich cultural experiences, delightful cuisines, stunning sights and fabulous shopping. These destinations are perfect for those looking to dive into the local vibe while enjoying their travel adventures.

Barcelona, Spain

Barcelona is a captivating city known for its unique blend of history, art and vibrant street life. The city is famous for its architecture, particularly the works of Antoni Gaudí.

Main attraction: Under construction for over a century, the iconic Sagrada Familia basilica symbolizes the city's artistic spirit.

Must-do activities: Stroll through the Gothic Quarter, visit Park Güell for whimsical sculptures and gardens, and savor tapas at local bars. Don't miss a visit to the Picasso Museum, which showcases the artist's early works in a beautiful setting.

Tips: The best time to visit is April to June and September to October when the weather is mild and crowds are smaller. To save money, consider purchasing a Barcelona Card for free public transport and discounts on major attractions.

Tokyo, Japan

Tokyo is a bustling metropolis that combines tradition and modernity. Ancient temples are nestled among cutting-edge skyscrapers, and the city offers a lively atmosphere and diverse experiences.

Main attraction: The historic Senso-ji Temple in Asakusa, Japan's oldest temple and a major cultural landmark.

Must-do activities: Visit Meiji Shrine, stroll in Harajuku for eclectic shops, and explore the culinary delights in Tsukiji Outer Market. Don't forget to relax in Ueno Park or enjoy views from the Tokyo Skytree.

Tips: The best time to visit is spring (March to May) for cherry blossoms or autumn (September to November) for beautiful fall foliage. To save money, consider purchasing a prepaid Suica or Pasmo card for easy public transport travel, and look for discount tickets for popular attractions.

Buenos Aires, Argentina

Also known as "The Paris of South America", Buenos Aires boasts a mix of European elegance and Latin passion, offering vibrant street life and a rich cultural scene.

Main attraction: The famous neighborhood of La Boca, known for its colorful buildings and street tango performances.

Must-do activities: Visit the historic Plaza de Mayo city square, stroll through the beautiful Recoleta Cemetery, and enjoy a tango show at a local milonga (tango venue). Don't miss trying traditional Argentine barbecue (asado).

Tips: The best time to visit is from September to November (spring) and March to May (fall) when temperatures are mild. Consider staying in an Airbnb for unique experiences and savings.

Prague, Czech Republic

With its stunning architecture and rich history, Prague is often called the "City of a Hundred Spires", offering beautiful sights in every direction.

Main attractions: The iconic Charles Bridge and Prague Castle, which overlook the Vltava River.

Must-do activities: Explore the Old Town Square, visit the astronomical clock, and enjoy scenic views from Petrin Hill. Take a stroll along the Vltava River and savor traditional Czech cuisine.

Tips: The best time to visit is from May to September when mild weather and outdoor festivals occur. Use the efficient public transport system to save money and seek out local pubs for budget-friendly dining.

Cape Town, South Africa

Cape Town is renowned for its breathtaking natural beauty, including Table Mountain and stunning coastlines. It's a vibrant cultural hub with diverse influences.

Main attraction: Table Mountain, offering panoramic views of the city and coastline.

Must-do activities: Take the cable car up Table Mountain, visit the historic Robben Island, and explore the vibrant V&A Waterfront. Enjoy the nearby beaches and the Cape Winelands for wine tasting.

Tips: For warm weather, the best time to visit is from October to April. To save money, consider using public transport or ride-sharing services for easy travel around the city.

Singapore

Singapore is a bustling, modern city-state known for its impressive skyline, multicultural population and lush greenery. It stands out as a global hub for finance, culture and tourism.

Main attraction: The stunning Marina Bay Sands complex featuring the iconic hotel with panoramic views of the city and "the largest rooftop infinity pool in the world".

Must-do activities: Explore Gardens by the Bay, in particular the Supertree Grove with its futuristic Supertree vertical gardens. Visit historic Chinatown and Little India, and stroll through the Botanic Gardens, a UNESCO World Heritage Site. Don't miss sampling the local street food at hawker centers to taste Singapore's diverse cuisines.

Tips: The best time to visit is from February to April when the weather is slightly cooler and drier. To save money, use the efficient public transportation system and consider the Singapore Tourist Pass for unlimited rides on buses and trains.

Kyoto, Japan

As the former imperial capital of Japan, Kyoto is renowned for its stunning temples, beautiful gardens and timeless traditions, offering a glimpse into Japan's rich cultural heritage.

Main attraction: The golden Kinkaku-ji (Golden Pavilion), a stunning Zen temple covered in gold leaf and surrounded by beautiful gardens.

Must-do activities: Visit Fushimi Inari Taisha with its thousands of vibrant torii gates, stroll through the Arashiyama Bamboo Grove, and explore the historic Gion district where you might glimpse a geisha. Don't miss the serene beauty of the Kiyomizu-dera Temple.

Tips: The best time to visit is spring (March to May) for cherry blossoms or autumn (September to November) for vibrant foliage. To save money, consider getting a Kyoto City Bus Card for unlimited travel on public transportation.

Shanghai, China

Shanghai is a dynamic metropolis epitomizing modern China while embracing its rich heritage. Known for its stunning skyline, diverse culture and vibrant energy, Shanghai is a must-visit city for travelers seeking excitement and history.

Main attraction: The iconic Bund, where historical colonial architecture meets the futuristic skyline of the Pudong district, offering picturesque views along the Huangpu River.

Must-do activities: Stroll along the Bund at sunset for breathtaking views, visit the beautiful Yu Garden with its traditional Chinese landscaping, and explore the Shanghai Museum to learn about the city's deep historical roots. Don't miss taking an exhilarating ride to the top of the Shanghai Tower, the tallest building in China, for unparalleled city views.

Tips: The best time to visit is spring (March to May) and fall (September to November) when the weather is mild and pleasant. Utilize the efficient public transportation system, including the metro, which is affordable and convenient. Look for dining options at local eateries or food markets to experience authentic Shanghai cuisine without breaking the bank.

CHAPTER 7
CRAFTING YOUR UNIQUE BUCKET LIST

Close your eyes and think of yourself standing at the edge of a vast, open field, the horizon stretching far and wide, filled with endless possibilities. That's what crafting your W.I.S.E. retirement bucket list is like—a canvas where you can paint your dreams, goals and aspirations with broad, sweeping strokes of creativity and intention. Whether you want to embark on a new hobby, connect with loved ones, or travel to places you've only seen on postcards, your bucket list is your manifesto for a life of purpose and joy.

To simplify the process for you, I've created a template planner on the next page that outlines all the essential components of the W.I.S.E. bucket list. Just fill in the blanks, and you're all set for the next step of the journey.

My W.I.S.E. Bucket List Planner

NAME

DATE

_____

_____

MY PURPOSE

MY PASSIONS

_____

_____

	W	**I**	**S**	**E**
	Warm the Heart	Invigorate the Mind	Strengthen the Body	Elevate the Soul
I want to...	1.	1.	1.	1.
	2.	2.	2.	2.
	3.	3.	3.	3.
	4.	4.	4.	4.

To help you navigate this journey, let me introduce you to the S.T.A.R. map:

Set goals
Tailor experiences
Adapt to changes
Refresh and review

This is your compass that ensures you stay on course while allowing for the spontaneity that makes life exciting. Try it.

Your S.T.A.R. Map

Grab a blank paper or open a new document on your computer. Draw four quadrants and label them:

Set Goals
Tailor Experiences
Adapt to Changes
Refresh and Review

In each section, jot down ideas, dreams and aspirations related to that theme. Let your thoughts flow freely, without judgment or constraints. Use this map as a living guide that evolves with your desires and discoveries, and revisit it often.

S: SET GOALS: BALANCING AMBITION WITH FEASIBILITY

My friend Juriah once told me that her retirement would be when she finally learned to play the saxophone, traveled to Paris, and started a small business hosting travelers in her home. It's exhilarating to dream big. But here's the catch—without a plan, dreams often remain just that: dreams. Setting achievable goals turns those dreams into realities.

Setting goals is the first step in the S.T.A.R. map. It's like deciding on your destination before setting sail. Identify your goal and give it shape and form. Goals give your life direction, transforming abstract desires into tangible milestones. They act as anchors, providing stability and focus amidst life's ever-changing waters. But remember, these goals are not set in stone. They are flexible and adaptable and meant to grow and evolve with you.

You want goals that stretch your imagination yet remain within the bounds of what you can realistically accomplish. To achieve this balance, consider what you genuinely wish to do and break those desires into smaller, manageable phases. If you tend to get overwhelmed easily, like me, it's helpful to set modest and achievable goals that edge you closer to your ultimate dreams. For instance, if your goal is to master digital graphic design, start by aiming to become proficient on user-friendly platforms like Canva, then target to ace intermediate tools such as Procreate or Affinity Designer, before aiming to deepen your skills in advanced programs like Adobe Illustrator or Photoshop.

Develop a step-by-step action plan to build a bridge from your current life to your dream retirement. For instance, if your goal is to travel to Paris, you might start by researching flights, learning a few French phrases, and setting aside a small amount of money each month to fund the trip. This approach makes the goal feel more attainable and keeps your motivation high by providing regular, tangible progress.

Setting timeframes and deadlines for each goal or milestone adds a sense of urgency and commitment. It's like marking the calendar for a dinner party—without a date, it's just a nice idea. But with a date, it becomes a plan you're excited to prepare for.

As you set out to achieve your goals, consider the resources and constraints that influence your plans. Assess your time, finances and physical abilities. You must know what's in your gas tank and how long you can drive without rest. Creating a budget for bucket list activities helps you understand what you can afford and where you might need to make adjustments. Perhaps you'll find that cutting back on dining out frees up funds for that saxophone you've been eyeing. Identifying support networks is equally important. Family and friends can offer encouragement and advice or join you on your adventures. Don't underestimate the power of a good pep talk when doubts creep in!

Evaluating progress is essential. Check in with yourself to see how far you've come and what's left to do. Using a goal-tracking app or journal can be a helpful way to stay organized and motivated. These tools act as a logbook, recording your achievements, challenges and adjustments. Regular monthly or quarterly review sessions allow you to reflect on what's working and what might need tweaking. It's like tending to a garden—sometimes, you must prune back the branches to make room for new growth. During these reviews, ask yourself: Are my goals still aligned with my values? Am I enjoying the process? These questions help ensure that your pursuits remain fulfilling and relevant.

While setting and pursuing goals, adaptability becomes your best friend. Life is unpredictable. Be flexible and allow for changes in location, timing or even the goals themselves. Your trip to Paris may be postponed due to unforeseen circumstances. Your interest in the saxophone wanes, and you discover a newfound passion for watercolor painting instead. Modifying goals based on health considerations is also key. Switching from marathon running to brisk walking is perfectly okay if that's what your body needs. Accept these shifts as natural parts of the journey, not as failures. Remember, the ultimate aim is to create a fulfilling retirement that feels right for you.

Balancing ambition with feasibility is about dreaming big while keeping your feet on the ground. As you set your goals and pursue them, cherish the process of learning, growing, and discovering new facets of yourself.

T: TAILOR EXPERIENCES: DESIGNING A PERSONALIZED ADVENTURE

What truly lights up your world? Tailor your W.I.S.E. bucket list to include experiences that resonate deeply with who you are and what you value. Tailoring experiences is where your creativity and individuality come into play. Whether you're learning a new language, diving into a creative pursuit, or exploring your local community, tailoring your adventures allows you to make more meaningful memories.

Self-reflection is your compass, guiding you toward activities that align with your interests and passions. You might consider journaling as a tool for self-discovery. It's like having a conversation with yourself on paper, where your thoughts and dreams can roam freely. Reflecting on childhood aspirations when the world seemed full of magic, can be enlightening. What did you want to be when you grew up? An astronaut, a painter, a world traveler? Understanding these early desires can explain what might still hold significance for you today. Align your bucket list with your values and let them guide you, whether it's sustainability, creativity or community. This ensures that your experiences have meaning and purpose.

In this deeply personal journey, we cannot overstate the value of unique experiences. You might want to create a personalized art piece, or organize a private family concert imbued with love and nostalgia. These moments transcend the ordinary, leaving an indelible mark on your heart. Rather than ticking off generic activities, aim for those that hold special meaning for you. You may want to host a gathering where your family recreates a beloved childhood tradition. Or create a scrapbook documenting your life's milestones, each page telling a story only you can tell. These experiences become part of your legacy, a testament to the life you've lived and the memories you've cherished.

It's a good idea to explore a variety of unique activities so that your bucket list is as diverse and multifaceted as you are. Consider attending a cultural festival in a different city, immersing yourself in the vibrant sights, sounds and flavors. What about participating in a themed retreat, where you can delve into a subject or hobby that fascinates you, surrounded by others who share your enthusiasm? These explorations broaden your horizons, introducing you to new perspectives. Keep your options open, and let curiosity guide you as you navigate the vast landscape of potential experiences.

There are tools and resources that can help tailor activities to your individual preferences. Online platforms offer personalized travel itineraries, allowing you to customize your adventures to the smallest detail. Whether finding a guided tour off the beaten path or locating a cooking class in Tuscany, the digital world is your oyster. Local workshops and courses on niche topics provide another avenue for crafting tailored experiences. These resources empower you to create a unique bucket list that reflects your tastes and aspirations.

But here's where prioritization comes in. With endless possibilities, focusing on what truly matters is crucial. Create a priority list to ensure you're dedicating your time and energy to the most significant pursuits. This might mean letting go of non-essential commitments and freeing yourself from obligations that no longer serve you. It's a process of distillation, where only the most meaningful experiences remain.

Tailor your bucket list to design a retirement that reflects your soul's desires. Let your imagination soar.

A: ADAPT TO CHANGES: EMBRACING FLEXIBILITY

Life sometimes springs a surprise and your plans go askew. But here's the good news: change is an opportunity, not an obstacle. Embracing flexibility in your retirement plans can be liberating. Adopt a mindset of resilience, where you learn to adapt to change rather than fight it. This mindset helps you adjust your sails to whatever winds come your way, ensuring that you continue moving forward, albeit on a different course than initially plotted.

Recognizing when a plan needs adjustment can save you from frustration. Listen to your intuition; it often knows when something isn't quite right. Maybe that long-awaited cruise gets rescheduled, or your new hobby isn't bringing you joy. That's okay! These are signs pointing you toward a new path. Building buffer time into your schedule is a practical way to accommodate these shifts. Also, have backup options for key activities so you're always prepared.

Embrace change with open arms, and it can lead to delightful surprises. For instance, a canceled trip might lead you to a chance encounter with spontaneous local events. Whether it's a pop-up art exhibit or a surprise farmers' market, these experiences can offer a refreshing change of pace. And don't shy away from last-minute travel deals. Sometimes, the best adventures are the ones you never saw coming, which force you to pack your bags on a whim and discover a new corner of the world. By staying open to these opportunities, you transform change into a friend, enriching your life with experiences you might have missed.

Yet, let's be honest—change can be harsh on the emotions. It's perfectly normal to feel a bit rattled when plans shift. Practicing mindfulness and stress management techniques can ground you during these times. Whether it's a few minutes of deep breathing, a calming walk in nature, or simply sipping a cup of tea, these moments of mindfulness can create a calm oasis in the storm of change. Engaging in these practices regularly can help you approach life's twists and turns with a more balanced perspective, allowing you to respond rather than react.

Remember, you don't have to navigate change alone. Seeking support from friends and family can make a world of difference. Sharing your feelings, concerns and excitement about new opportunities can lighten your emotional load. Your loved ones can offer perspectives you hadn't considered, and their encouragement can boost your confidence as you adapt to new circumstances. Sometimes, knowing that someone is in your corner can reassure you to face change with courage and grace.

Adapting to changes is not just a skill; it's a way of life. Approach retirement with creativity and an open mind, and allow yourself to flow with the currents. While the path may meander, the journey can still lead you to incredible destinations. So, as you craft your retirement bucket list, remember to leave room for the unexpected. After all, some of life's best moments come from the plans we never made, the paths we never intended to walk.

R: REFRESH AND REVIEW: REVISITING AND UPDATING YOUR LIST

View your bucket list as a living document, alive, growing and evolving—much like you are. Revisit your list regularly, ensuring it remains relevant and inspiring. Life is dynamic, and so, too, should be your bucket list. Take the time to celebrate your achievements, reflect on your experiences, and adjust as needed. This step is about keeping the zest alive, ensuring that your list continues to motivate and excite you. It's a reminder that life is an ongoing adventure, and there's always more to explore and discover.

As you tick off completed milestones, take a moment to celebrate. Commemorate them with a small personal ritual, whether it's a toast with loved ones or a reflective walk in the park. These moments of joy add depth to your journey, making each accomplishment a cherished memory.

Keeping your enthusiasm high requires a bit of creativity. Joining online communities can provide a steady source of inspiration and camaraderie. These groups are like bustling marketplaces, full of shared experiences and fresh ideas that can reignite your passion. Not only do they offer support, but they also remind you that you're not alone in your pursuits. Documenting your adventures is another way to keep the spark alive. Whether through photography, scrapbooking or journaling, capturing these moments allows you to relive and share them with others. It's like creating a time capsule, preserving the essence of your experiences for future reflection. These records become treasured keepsakes, allowing you to revisit your adventures and draw inspiration from them as you plan new ones.

Periodic reflection and reassessment are necessary pauses that offer perspective. Conduct an annual bucket list review to reflect on your accomplishments and where you want to go next. It's a moment to step back and evaluate whether your list still excites and motivates you. Don't hesitate to ask for feedback from family and peers. Sometimes, an outside perspective can offer insights you hadn't considered, guiding you toward more meaningful and attainable objectives. These conversations can help refine your goals and perhaps even discover new interests. As you reassess, remember that your list reflects your current self, and it's perfectly okay for it to change as you do.

Marking significant achievements and moments with milestone events or gatherings can be immensely rewarding. Whether it's a small dinner with close friends or a grand celebration with family, these events honor your journey and the milestones you've reached. They offer an opportunity to share your successes, express gratitude, and strengthen your connections with loved ones. Consider creating a legacy project to leave behind—a scrapbook, a video montage, or even a family recipe book. These projects preserve your stories and memories for future generations.

An example of transformative reflection is my cousin Benjamin. Upon retirement from the Navy, he turned his career achievements into a personal museum, curating a collection of memorabilia that tells the story of his naval adventures. With each piece, he reflects on the milestones and lessons learned. We were proud to know he had experienced and achieved so much in life.

Then there's cousin Stephanie, who at 57, hosted an annual reflection night with friends, where they gathered to share life lessons and support each other's dreams. She's still at it today! These gatherings have become a source of inspiration and encouragement for herself and participants, reinforcing the bonds of friendship. Steph's and Ben's stories illustrate the power of reflection and celebration in enriching our lives and deepening our understanding of ourselves.

As you refresh and review your W.I.S.E. bucket list, nurture it with the same care and attention you give to the most critical aspects of your life. Remember that your bucket list is a living testament to your dreams, ready to evolve and grow alongside you.

INSPIRE OTHERS: YOUR VOICE MATTERS

Now that you have all the tools to enjoy a vibrant and enriching retirement, it's time to share your newfound insights and guide others on their journey.

By taking a moment to leave your honest review of this book on Amazon, you can help fellow retirees and those approaching retirement find the valuable information they need. Your words can inspire others to embrace their retirement with enthusiasm and purpose.

Thank you for being a part of this adventure. The spirit of a fulfilling retirement lives on when we share what we've learned—and you're making that happen!

Scan the QR code to leave your review on Amazon:

CONCLUSION

Well, here we are at the end of our journey together. I hope you've found this book as much of an adventure as I've enjoyed writing it! I wanted to offer insights that resonate with your personal experiences and aspirations. This perspective has been my guiding star, ensuring the advice and ideas are relatable, practical and tailored to you. I hope I have achieved that.

Let's take a moment to reflect on the path we've traveled. We've explored the heart of retirement with a holistic, budget-friendly approach, focusing on purposeful adventures, deeper connections, and vibrant living. The aim is to transform retirement from a passive phase into an exciting and significant chapter of life.

As we wrap up, let's revisit some key pointers:

- Retirement is a golden opportunity to rediscover your passions and purpose. It's a time to embrace new roles and identities, from mentoring to volunteering to enjoying hobbies that bring you joy.
- Maintaining a vibrant and fulfilling retirement lifestyle doesn't have to break the bank. With some creativity, you can explore the world, learn new skills, and connect with others—all while staying within your budget.
- Dream big, but start small, and watch your dreams become reality. Then, take action with enthusiasm and intention to reach that goal.

Thank you for joining me on this journey. Your willingness to explore, dream and plan has brought you so far and is an achievement in itself. I invite you to continue engaging with the community because you're not alone in this adventure. Consider joining discussion groups, attending workshops, or sharing your stories and experiences. Your participation and input can inspire others just as theirs can inspire you. You can also connect with me at elizagolding27@gmail.com. Let's keep the conversation going and support one another as we craft the retirement of our dreams.

Here's to you and the adventures that await. May your days be filled with laughter, your heart with joy, and your bucket list with experiences that light up your soul.

REFERENCES

How to smoothly navigate the identity-changing transition into retirement. (n.d.). The Week. https://theweek.com/articles/829190/how-smoothly-navigate-identitychanging-transition-into-retirement

Rabbitt, T. (n.d.). Reinventing retirement: How to thrive with purpose and passion. LinkedIn. https://www.linkedin.com/pulse/reinventing-retirement-how-thrive-purpose-passion-thomas-rabbitt-r65de

Discover the benefits of mentoring for seniors. (n.d.). Harmony Home Health. https://www.harmonyhomehealth.com/the-benefits-of-mentoring-for-seniors/

The benefits of lifelong learning for older adults. (n.d.). UNESCO Institute for Lifelong Learning. https://www.uil.unesco.org/en/thematic-studies-benefits-lifelong-learning-older-adults

Living well: Nine holistic approaches to senior health. (n.d.). Presbyterian Homes. https://www.presbyterianhomes.org/blog/holistic-approaches-to-senior-health/#:

Retire Wise launches innovative coaching program for a fulfilling retirement. (n.d.). Yahoo Finance. https://finance.yahoo.com/news/retire-wise-launches-innovative-coaching-141700110.html

The importance of social engagement and how to promote it among older adults. (n.d.). Chen Medical Centers. https://www.chenmedicalcenters.com/articles/importance-social-engagement-and-how-promote-it-among-older-adults

8 senior social clubs that you should be joining. (n.d.). The Arbor Company. https://www.arborcompany.com/blog/8-senior-social-clubs-that-you-should-be-joining

Intergenerational activity ideas for seniors and youth to do together. (n.d.). Institute on Aging. https://www.ioaging.org/senior-socialization/intergenerational-activity-ideas-for-seniors-and-youth-to-do-together/

Online communities for seniors: How to find friends online. (n.d.). Senior Lifestyle. https://www.seniorlifestyle.com/resources/blog/virtual-communities-for-seniors/

Continuing education for seniors: How to take advantage of lifelong learning. (n.d.). Institute on Aging. https://www.ioaging.org/activities-well

ness/continuing-education-for-seniors-how-to-take-advantage-of-lifelong-learning/

5 sites with online classes for seniors to keep learning. (n.d.). Center for a Secure Retirement. https://www.centerforasecureretirement.com/posts/5-sites-with-online-classes-for-seniors-to-keep-learning

Foreign language training as cognitive therapy for age-related cognitive decline. (n.d.). National Institutes of Health. https://pmc.ncbi.nlm.nih.gov/articles/PMC3890428/

Best brain and memory games for dementia. (n.d.). Healthline. https://www.healthline.com/health/alzheimers-dementia/memory-games-for-dementia#:~

Physical activity benefits for adults 65 or older. (n.d.). Centers for Disease Control and Prevention. https://www.cdc.gov/physical-activity-basics/health-benefits/older-adults.html#:~

Best sports for older adults, according to experts. (n.d.). Forbes. https://www.forbes.com/health/healthy-aging/best-sports-for-older-adults/

Healthy eating, nutrition, and diet. (n.d.). National Institute on Aging. https://www.nia.nih.gov/health/healthy-eating-nutrition-and-diet

Time in nature may help older adults with improved health and purpose in life. (n.d.). Penn State University. https://www.psu.edu/news/health-and-human-development/story/time-nature-may-help-older-adults-improved-health-purpose-life

Five ways to give your retirement purpose. (n.d.). Kiplinger. https://www.kiplinger.com/retirement/ways-to-give-your-retirement-purpose

20 secret places in Florida that only locals know. (n.d.). Southern Living. https://www.southernliving.com/travel/florida/best-secret-places-visit-fl?srsltid=AfmBOorMCndvrdGgHXj_qIn2u-_0Cx1unFLLJa-mwD8zf bFVxCk3SSwD

KOA. (n.d.). *7 tips for RVing on a budget*. KOA Camping Blog. https://koa.com/blog/rving-on-a-budget/

Volunteer Forever. (n.d.). *How to volunteer abroad ethically (and avoid scams)*. https://www.volunteerforever.com/article_post/how-to-volunteer-abroad-ethically-and-avoid-scams/

Bayntree. (n.d.). *Holistic retirement planning: 5 tips for a balanced, fulfilling retirement*. https://www.bayntree.com/financial-advice/holistic-retirement-planning-5-tips-for-a-balanced-fulfilling-retirement

Advisor Magazine. (n.d.). *Adapting to the new retirement.* https://www.lifehealth.com/adapting-to-the-new-retirement/

U.S. News & World Report. (n.d.). *6 common retirement goals | aging.* https://money.usnews.com/money/retirement/aging/articles/common-retirement-goals

Adult Enrichment Centers. (n.d.). *The benefits of journaling for seniors.* https://www.adultenrichmentcenters.org/blog/the-benefits-of-journaling-for-seniors/

Vernon, S. (2023, June 23). *What is retirement resilience – and how can you build it?.* Forbes. https://www.forbes.com/sites/stevevernon/2023/06/23/what-is-retirement-resilience-and-how-can-you-build-it/

Positive Psychology. (n.d.). *Positive aging: 10+ principles to shift beliefs around age.* https://positivepsychology.com/positive-aging/

Eden Senior Healthcare. (n.d.). *The role of optimism in improving mental health for seniors.* https://www.edenseniorhc.com/the-role-of-optimism-in-improving-mental-health-for-seniors/#:~:

Pappas, E., & Kuhl, D. (2020). Sense of purpose in life and five health behaviors in older adults. *PMC7494628.* https://pmc.ncbi.nlm.nih.gov/articles/PMC7494628/

Mayo Clinic. (n.d.). *Friendships: Enrich your life and improve your health.* https://www.mayoclinic.org/healthy-lifestyle/adult-health/in-depth/friendships/art-20044860

Wells, W. (2020). Social connection as a critical factor for health in older adults. *PMC11403199.* https://pmc.ncbi.nlm.nih.gov/articles/PMC11403199/

The Renew Center. (n.d.). *Unlock mental clarity: The power of journaling.* https://www.therenewcenter.com/blogs/unlock-mental-clarity-the-power-of-journaling

C3A. (n.d.). *Retirees with a sense of purpose do better.* https://www.c3a.org.sg/articles/retirees-sense-purpose-do-better

ACKNOWLEDGMENTS

To my husband Michael,

Thank you for standing by me throughout this writing journey. You've been my sounding board, pace-setter, financier, coffee runner, morale booster... And your honesty about the cover? Critical but appreciated. Thanks for your unwavering belief, and for always cheering me on. This book is for you.